Advances using AI – The Next Wave

Editors

Vanamali Somanchi

Richard R. Khan

Tulay Guneysel

Advances using AI – The Next Wave

Beyond the Hype: A Guide to the Quiet Revolution

What does 'Generative AI' truly mean? Is it a tool, partner, or rival? In a world filled with stories of digital artists and all-knowing virtual assistants, it is easy to feel caught between wonder and worry. The 'thought of fear' – the quiet anxiety that our human roles could be replaced – is a natural response to technology that is advancing at a breathtaking pace.

However, what if we are asking the wrong question?

We believe that the real revolution is not happening on our screens but is unfolding silently and invisibly in the spaces between our thoughts and tasks. It is in this spirit that we have brought together nine distinct voices – researchers, engineers, and strategists – to explore this 'Revolutionary Evolution.' This book is an invitation to look beyond the hype and the fear and to consider a more hopeful and productive future: a hybrid world where our organic selves and our technological creations work in harmony, not in conflict.

Forget dense jargon. Through these insightful chapters, you will discover how AI is already helping to decipher our emotions, making quality education accessible to remote villages, and ensuring that our technology remains sustainable and green. Each chapter is a journey into a different part of this new world, challenging our assumptions and revealing the human-centric potential of these powerful tools. We envision a future where AI's purpose is not to replace us but to assist with the ordinary so we can focus on what truly matters: creativity, critical thinking, and connection.

This book is a guide that offers clarity and confidence for our shared journey ahead. It is for the student, the professional, the parent, and the curious citizen who want to understand this technology for what it is, appreciate its worth, and learn to move forward with it, keeping in stride. This proves that progress does not have to be a zero-sum game. We can build a world where technology gives us efficiency, and in return, we give ourselves the space to create, reflect, and simply be without the pressure of racing against the machine.

Join us in this exploration. Let us move past the fear of replacement and, together, begin composing the next chapter of the human story.

Advances using AI – The Next Wave

Editors

Vanamali Somanchi

Richard R. Khan

Tulay Guneysel

Advances using AI – The Next Wave

First edition published 2026

by CRC Press

2385 NW Executive Center Drive, Suite 320, Boca Raton FL 33431

and by CRC Press

4 Park Square, Milton Park, Abingdon, Oxon, OX14 4RN

CRC Press is an imprint of Taylor & Francis Group, LLC

Designed cover image: Shutterstock

For Product Safety Concerns and Information please contact our EU representative GPSR@taylorandfrancis.com. Taylor & Francis Verlag GmbH, Kaufingerstraße 24, 80331 München, Germany.

Library of Congress Cataloging-in-Publication Data

ISBN: 9781041236993 (hbk)
ISBN: 9781003737803 (ebk)
ISBN: 9781041237402 (pbk)
DOI: 10.1201/9781003737803

Publisher's note: This book has been prepared from camera-ready copy provided by the authors.

This book is dedicated to

our parents, teachers and all those

who influence and support

our journeys as life-long learners.

Foreword by GGU

Golden Gate University Worldwide is proud to be an integral part of this brilliant scholar-practitioner book, which is reflective of our leadership and service mission. As our DBA in Emerging Technology, GenAI students, the authors invested countless hours in and out of our classrooms listening, debating, applying, researching, and reflecting on an emerging, evolving, and disruptive technology that has become pivotal to our global society. Throughout their discussions and debates, the authors, as participant observers, noted a striking gap: while headlines oscillated between alarm and awe, the true complexity of Generative AI was often distilled into simple narratives, sometimes minimizing its potential, other times overstating its threats.

As their conversations deepened, so too did their realization that Generative AI models like BERT and ChatGPT signaled a watershed moment, moving AI from the periphery of academia into mainstream consciousness and utilization. These advances generated a mix of excitement and apprehension, underscoring the widening chasm between public perception and the nuanced realities of AI's capabilities, limitations, and societal responsibility. It quickly became clear to them, their professors, and their classmates that something new was needed – a scholar-practitioner volume that would bridge this gap and spur further dialogue, debate, and validation.

Hence, as thought leaders, our bold DBA student-authors developed *Advances Using AI – The Next Wave*, as their collective contribution to bridging the gap and continuing the dialogue. As global servants, they are generously donating proceeds from the book to charity.

We salute you!

Stay focused,

Jay Gonzalez, PhD

Vice Provost for Global Affairs and Founding Dean

Mick McGee, DPA

Associate Dean and DBA Director

Foreword by upGrad

On behalf of upGrad, I am delighted to present *Advances Using AI – The Next Wave*, a collective initiative by our Doctoral students.

Generative AI has moved swiftly from the realm of academic research into the centre of public discourse. Yet, much of this discourse oscillates between extremes – either boundless optimism about its potential or deep concern over its implications. This book seeks to provide a more balanced view. It invites readers to move beyond polarized narratives and to see AI for what it truly is: a powerful enabler that, when harnessed responsibly, can amplify human creativity, insight, and impact.

At upGrad, we believe education must go beyond equipping learners with knowledge; it must prepare them to navigate uncertainty with confidence and adaptability. Learning is not confined to classrooms or courses – it is an ongoing journey, powered by curiosity, relevance, and application. This publication, conceptualized and edited by our DBA students, embodies that philosophy. It illustrates how learners, through academic rigor and practical perspective, can transform ideas into contributions of real-world significance.

The strength of this work lies in its diversity of perspectives. Spanning nine chapters, the authors explore how AI is reshaping domains such as education, healthcare, sustainability, and the creative industries. Collectively, these chapters affirm a core principle: AI is not here to replace human capability, but to complement it. By automating the routine, it empowers us to devote greater energy to what defines us most – imagination, collaboration, and meaningful human connection.

This book is more than an academic endeavour. It is a contribution to the ongoing global dialogue on responsible technology adoption and its profound implications for business, society, and human progress. It underscores our commitment at upGrad to lifelong learning and to fostering critical engagement with emerging technologies.

We hope that *Advances Using AI – The Next Wave* inspires students, professionals, and all curious minds to approach the evolving landscape of AI with both confidence and responsibility.

Regards,

Sandeep Pereira,

Delivery Director,

upGrad International

Preface

The concept for this book came about as many great things do, through active conversation. As doctoral students sharing our pursuits in Generative Artificial Intelligence (Gen AI), we listened, shared, argued, and debated about a technology that not only was central to our work but was also influencing the world beyond academics. We watched the headlines and saw a mixed bag of public awareness and concern. We were equally taken aback by how often the deep complexity of Artificial Intelligence (AI) was flattened into simple stories or, at other times, blown out of proportion.

Soon, as our conversations gained momentum, we began to see that this was no longer simply a passing fancy. Yes, artificial intelligence has existed since the early waves of information technology (IT). Still, generative models like BERT, ChatGPT, and the like, presented a tipping point, bringing AI from relative obscurity into the center of public conversation. These models, which could ingest a myriad of stores of human knowledge and produce content anew, created both excitement and anxiety. Amidst growing turmoil, we began to see a widening gap: the real capabilities and potential benefits of AI, contrasted with simplistic, at times sensational, media stories.

Advances Using AI – The Next Wave is our collective attempt to fill that gap. Each chapter contemplates revolutionary evolution and considers the implications of AI in fields such as education, healthcare, creativity, recreation, and at the heart of it all, the human themes of hope and uncertainty. Writing this book has been both an intellectual exercise and an expression of service. This book represents our way of "giving back". It is our small contribution to the larger conversation about AI. As part of that service, we have agreed to donate all proceeds from this book to charity, honoring the support we have received from our teachers, mentors, and communities along the way.

We are very much aware that the book is captured only a moment in time. AI, a colloquial alternative for Gen AI, is moving quickly and what we debate today might appear as different tomorrow. Nevertheless, we hope to capture our reflections and facilitate a springboard for future voices to join in mapping the changing story of what AI means for humanity, both at work and in spirit – your voice included.

We want to thank all those great souls that supported us along the journey – our mentors, our education institutions, and our communities. And, of course, we want to thank you for being willing to engage in these ideas. We hope the pages ahead will help to counsel, inspire and prepare you for the determinative future ahead – what will be the next wave of AI, which is already upon us.

Table of Contents

AI for Rural-Classrooms to Industry-Skilling

By Abhay Tewari*

Introduction

The dual forces of education and enterprise have helped shape the character and success of the society. While education helps people with knowledge and the ability to think critically, the industry or enterprise helps transform that knowledge into productive action serving communities or addressing global challenges. These two forces have operated together in parallel for centuries: schools and colleges taught theory, while businesses put them into practice. However, in this era of extraordinary technological change, the distance between the classroom and the boardroom seems widening. This gap is especially visible in countries like India, where millions of students in rural and semi-urban areas lack access to high-quality teachers, mentors, or role models[6,8]. At the

---

*· Abhay Tewari is an Actuary, Data Scientist, and Investment Specialist whose career bridges the worlds of quantitative science and strategic leadership. As MD & CEO of Star Union Dai-ichi Life Insurance, he applies data-driven decision-making to create value for customers, distributors, and shareholders, while advancing sustainable growth in insurance penetration across India.

DOI: 10.1201/9781003737803-1

same time, industries in the country are transforming at a speed that challenges even experienced professionals. With nearly 65% of its 1.4 billion population below the age of 35, India is the youngest large nation in the world[1]. This demographic dividend can be the greatest strength for the country, giving it the potential to power global supply chains, fuel innovation, and emerge as one of the largest consumer and producer markets. Yet, the same youth advantage can become a liability without access to quality education, meaningful skilling, and pathways to dignified employment. This tension, between promise and peril, defines the urgency of reimagining education and training in India.

At the heart of the problem lies the deep divide between urban and rural education. The cities have good schools and colleges, often equipped with advanced laboratories, experienced faculty, and strong industry linkages. In contrast, the villages in India struggle with schools that lack qualified teachers, have minimal infrastructure, and rely on outdated curricula with subpar quality. The second issue is the relevance of the content since there is a huge mismatch between education in schools and colleges and industry requirements[3,4]. What students learn often lags what industries demand, and what industries demand is often unknown to students until they enter the workforce. This is true even for the better-funded schools and universities, as curricula are slow to adapt to the skill requirements of different industries, and there is a gap in the problem-solving and creative thinking required to meet the business challenges. The consequence is a mismatch: industries struggle to find job-ready talent, while millions of youngsters struggle to find jobs and remain unemployed or underemployed.

Traditional approaches of building more schools, hiring more teachers, or setting up new training centres are necessary. However, despite enormous resources and time investment in such facilities, they remain insufficient, with many learners still excluded. This is where artificial intelligence (AI) offers unprecedented possibilities to change how we tell stories, train people, and spread knowledge[5,9,13]. Artificial intelligence is moving from being the domain of researchers to becoming a useful tool for creators, entrepreneurs, and educators. It is becoming increasingly capable in generating lifelike voices, animating characters, creating immersive storylines, and delivering personalized tutoring. What was once the domain of large film studios, high-quality animation, photorealistic character rendering, dubbing in multiple languages, can now be accomplished on a laptop using tools that cost less than a single day of traditional filming. And this isn't just about cost-cutting; it allows creators to experiment endlessly, adapt content to different audiences, and bring visions to life without logistical barriers. A good AI-powered platform can generate hundreds of video lessons in multiple languages, simulate real-world business scenarios, and adapt or personalize the explanations based on the learner's pace and comprehension. It can reach the remotest corners of India through smartphones[4, 6].

However, many e-learning initiatives in the past have failed because they treated digital lessons as mere replicas of textbooks, dry, one-way information transmission. To truly engage with learners, our content must not only be about sharing information but also about engaging and inspiring. The AI-powered storytelling can help put complex concepts into relatable narratives – through short videos, films, or animated comics, AI can make education accessible and enjoyable. For instance, the physics concepts like motion or energy could be explained through relatable scenarios, such as a farmer using a bullock cart or a child flying a kite. The school lessons generated by AI can be tailored to relate to people's lives. The same concept applies to industry-specific training. A young professional entering the banking sector might find it difficult to understand the processes only through written training materials. However, if the content is explained through an engaging AI-generated short film, where a family navigates a bank loan, an insurance policy, or a digital payment system it may be much easier to understand and retain the knowledge. From the epics like the Ramayana and the Mahabharata in India to the fables of Aesop in Greece, stories have served as the oldest form of education. They help teach values, explain complex truths, and inspire action. AI tools like video generators, voice synthesis platforms, animation models, and knowledge graphs are powerful and allow us to return to this storytelling mode of teaching.

This dual blueprint, of rural education and industry skilling, forms the backbone of this chapter. On one side is the aspiration to bring quality education to every child, regardless of geography. On the other hand, there is the ambition to equip youth and working professionals with the industry-relevant skills needed for meaningful employment and entrepreneurship. The two are not separate but complementary: without foundational education, skilling programs lack depth; without advanced skilling, education risks becoming irrelevant at least from the industry viewpoint. The chapter serves as an invitation to reimagine how India, and indeed the world, might grow if education and skilling were democratized through AI.

However, such a vision also raises questions about whether AI can truly replace the empathy and intuition of a teacher or mentor. Will students treat the animated lessons as mere entertainment? How do we ensure that industries portrayed in AI-generated stories are accurate, fair, and free of bias? What ethical safeguards are needed when using the likeness or voice of real individuals in AI-generated videos or films? Questions around consent, privacy, and intellectual property need to be considered. There is a possibility that the datasets being used to train the models may be biased[11,12]. Also, the cost of deploying AI tools may create a new division between those who can afford them and those who cannot. These questions do not diminish the idea's potential, but they cannot be ignored. We must address them openly, not as afterthoughts, but as integral parts of the design.

The following pages will expand this vision into concrete sections: first by laying out the dual blueprint of rural education and industry training, then by describing the technological ecosystem that makes such storytelling possible. We will move on to applications, explore the ethical and leadership dimensions, examine the challenges, and only propose a roadmap for implementation. It is worth noting that India is not alone in facing these challenges. Many of the emerging economies, including countries in Southeast Asia, Latin America, and most countries in Africa, grapple with similar issues of building scale with quality. Thus, the model for democratizing education and training we explore here is replicable globally. AI-powered storytelling can catalyze a more skilled, ethical, and prosperous India, and by extension, a more just and hopeful world. In the following pages, we will explore the two interwoven blueprints: one focused on empowering rural education through AI-powered teachers and storytellers, and the other focused on enabling industry-specific training through AI-driven videos, movies, and simulations. By addressing both sides of the spectrum, grassroots learning and professional skilling, we can create a pipeline of human potential that is future ready.

To summarize, the introduction lays out three critical ideas: The urgency to reimagine education and skilling in a country where the demographic dividend could otherwise become a demographic burden, the potential for AI-powered storytelling to bridge the education and skill gap, through new delivery models, with better explanation of difficult concepts or skills, which otherwise could only be mastered at the workplace and finally, the commitment to values and ethics ensuring that technology serves humanity rather than undermines it.

The Dual Blueprint: Education for All, Skills for the Future

India's transformation into a knowledge-driven economy will not happen by chance; it must be designed with care, foresight, and bold experimentation. At the center of this design lies what we may call the Dual Blueprint. This twin-track approach simultaneously addresses the foundational crisis of rural education and the advanced demands of industry-specific skilling.

While these two domains may appear separate, they are deeply interrelated. Without adequate exposure to mathematics, science, or language skills, village children cannot easily participate in high-value skilling programs later in life. Conversely, even the most well-educated youth may not be able to apply their knowledge without some kind of practical understanding of the needs of industry. Thus, the Dual Blueprint envisions education as a continuum: from developing the theoretical and conceptual foundation at the school and university level to specialized technical and leadership training for young professionals so that they are well prepared to meet the requirements and challenges of the industry.

Rural Education: Building the Foundation

The first pillar of the blueprint is to ensure that every child in rural India has access to engaging, high-quality, and contextually relevant education. Traditional classroom instruction depends on teacher availability and quality, so it often struggles in rural areas with scarce resources. AI storytelling offers a way to augment the available teachers, through ready-to-use video modules in local languages that can be delivered via smartphones, tablets, projectors, or even low-cost televisions. Storytelling is particularly effective because it can anchor abstract concepts by relating them to real-life experiences. For example, a module on renewable energy can showcase a farmer installing solar panels to power a water pump. The AI-generated stories can also adapt dynamically so that if a student struggles with the concepts, the AI tutor can pause, re-explain, or give other examples. If another student master's the topic quickly, the module can suggest additional exercises or puzzles. AI becomes a patient companion teacher, able to adjust to the diverse learning speeds in every classroom. Importantly, such content can be produced at scale, and a single AI storyteller platform can churn out hundreds of hours of localized video lessons in different dialects, ensuring inclusivity[4,6]. The mathematics module can be available in Marathi for Maharashtra, Bhojpuri for Bihar, and Kannada for Karnataka, each retaining cultural nuances while teaching the same universal concepts.

Industry-Ready Skills: Better employability and enterprise

Unlike general education, this skilling must be highly contextualized to the specific demands of sectors like financial services, energy, healthcare, information technology, electronics, manufacturing, or sports. Here too, storytelling proves invaluable. Industry training manuals are often long, technical, and uninspiring. But they come alive when reframed as narratives, short films, comic strips, or interactive modules. A short AI-generated film could depict a small-town entrepreneur seeking a loan, highlighting the steps of customer handling, due diligence, and risk assessment[3,4]. Instead of memorizing abstract compliance rules, bank trainees learn them in action. A simulation to explain technical concepts, like load balancing, in renewable energy, alongside soft skills, like collaboration could be done through a video showing a village cooperative installing wind turbines[6]. A comic series could dramatize the workflow of a rural clinic, teaching nurses about hygiene, triage, and digital health recordkeeping[8]. AI films might illustrate how athletes are recruited, trained, and sponsored, how the sporting events are marketed, giving aspiring managers a clear view of industry dynamics[5]. The skilling content must be regularly updated in consultation with employers so that it remains relevant.

Finally, while both blueprints have been mentioned in the Indian context, their lessons are global. Countries worldwide face similar gaps in education and skilling of the children, thus not preparing them for the workplace. By demonstrating how AI storytelling can address education and skill gaps, India can pioneer a model that many other countries can adapt. The Dual Blueprint thus represents not just a policy framework but a vision of hope, one where no child is too remote to learn, and no youth is too underprepared to aspire. It embodies the belief that education and skilling are not parallel tracks but a single highway toward empowerment.

The Technology Ecosystem

The ambitious vision of using AI-powered storytelling for rural education and industry-specific skilling can only succeed if a good technology ecosystem supports it. This ecosystem is not a single platform or product but an interlinked network of tools, processes, and partnerships that enable content creation, personalization, distribution, and feedback.

If the Dual Blueprint represents the what of the strategy, then the Technology Ecosystem represents the how. It answers the fundamental question: How can we scale high-quality, context-specific, multi-lingual storytelling to millions of learners across India, many of whom live in resource-constrained environments? The answer lies in building an ecosystem with five interlocking layers: Content Generation, Personalization Engines, Multi-lingual Infrastructure, Distribution Channels, and Data & Feedback Loops. Together, these layers form the digital spine of the AI-powered skilling revolution.

Content Generation: The Story Factory

At the heart of the ecosystem is the content that AI can generate, including relevant stories, videos, simulations, and other interactive modules. Unlike traditional textbooks, which take many years to update, AI storytelling platforms can generate new and relevant content using Large Language Models (LLMs) in days or even hours. Generative AI tools, including text-to-video systems like Runway or HeyGen, image generators like MidJourney, and voice synthesis engines like ElevenLabs, can be combined to create polished multimedia lessons[9, 13]. for Animation & Editing, Runway ML, Pika, DaVinci Resolve can be great tools. For the comic book version, we can use tools like Midjourney or Leonardo AI to generate consistent characters. Tools like Comic Life or Clip Studio Paint can help arrange and add dialogue. NovelAI and other such tools can help in creating interconnected, inspiring stories.

Such storytelling can follow predefined reusable templates, showing the competitive advantages in the industry, supply chain efficiencies, cost efficiencies, people skills, or others like distribution strengths or capital, which make some companies successful, whereas others may struggle. The idea is to help people understand what the industry needs and how successful businesses are not only about technical efficiencies and prowess but also about good leadership and values that set the organisation apart.

While AI can help produce the content, subject matter experts (teachers, industry professionals) should refine it and approve the final modules. This approach ensures more accuracy and precision. For example, a lesson on banking may begin with an AI-generated animation of a rural entrepreneur opening an account, accompanied by visuals of the local town. However, before finalisation, the whole content is vetted by a seasoned banker[3, 4].

This content factory approach can produce hundreds of modules per month, covering everything from explaining fractions to advanced risk assessment techniques.

Personalization Engines: Tailoring the Journey

AI can help personalize the content. In rural India, classrooms may have students with widely varying abilities. Similarly, the skilling programs often enroll participants with different knowledge levels. Personalization engines can incorporate adaptive assessments, wherein the system administers quick diagnostic tests before a student begins. Based on the results, the difficulty and pace of modules are adjusted[3,5]. If a learner struggles with say a module on compound interest, the AI storyteller can reframe the lesson with simpler analogies, perhaps using local farming examples. If they progress quickly, the system introduces advanced challenges, thus there is a dynamic adaptation and through recommendation engines the AI tutors can suggest the "next best lesson" based on learner history. For example, a rural child who enjoys stories involving sports might receive math lessons wrapped in cricket or kabaddi narratives. Personalization can engage the learners better and thereby reduce the dropout rates.

Multi-lingual Infrastructure: Training in one's language

India's language diversity creates a few additional challenges. While English and Hindi dominate higher education, true inclusivity requires content in local languages and dialects. Textual content must be available in multiple scripts (Devanagari, Tamil, Bengali, etc.), with seamless toggling. A farmer's son in Odisha may understand concepts more clearly in Odia than in Hindi. Neural Machine Translation (NMT) like Google translate can help translate the technical terms accurately while preserving the cultural context[12]. The latest AI voice engines can generate speech not just in Hindi but also in various local accents or dialects of Hindi like Maithili, Chhattisgarhi, or Bundeli, ensuring relatability[11]. In real life, many Indians mix English with their mother tongue ("Hinglish," "Tanglish"). It ensures that no learner feels handicapped or left out due to language barriers.

Distribution Channels: Reaching the Last Mile

Even the best content is useless if it cannot reach learners. Distribution is especially challenging in rural India, where internet penetration and electricity remain patchy. The technology ecosystem must therefore be channel-agnostic and resilient. With nearly 700 million smartphone users in India, mobile-first content is critical. Lightweight apps with offline caching allow downloading videos and quizzes when connectivity is available. Community Digital Hubs can be created in Panchayat halls, or libraries, where projectors or low-cost tablets are shared amongst learners. While AI-generated films should have mobile phone users as their main target, they can be repurposed for television or radio, extending reach to households without smartphones[4,6]. For youth skilling campaigns, simple storytelling modules can be circulated as WhatsApp videos or Instagram reels. The local banks branches can be partnered to host financial literacy and industry skilling videos in their branches, while schools can be encouraged to integrate AI modules into regular classes. This multi-channel strategy ensures the ubiquity of access through a personal phone, a shared hub, or even a broadcast medium.

Data & Feedback Loops: Continuous Improvement

The final layer of the ecosystem is the feedback mechanism. AI-driven learning is not static; it thrives on data. Every interaction, clicks, pauses, wrong answers, or questions asked, provides insights. The data, with analytics, feedback, and refinement, can bring continuous improvement. There can be dashboards or analytics for teachers and administrators showing how many students completed modules, which topics were difficult, and where dropouts occurred. The AI Tutor can be enabled to build a memory profile of the strengths and weaknesses for each learner, which helps the lessons to be customized and improve over time. There can be system of community feedback, wherein villagers and learners can report whether stories felt authentic, translations worked, or examples were culturally mismatched. For skilling, employers can give feedback on whether trainees were adequately prepared, feeding back into module design.

Thus, the data cycle, followed by feedback and refinement, ensures the content stays relevant, effective, and engaging. Each layer does not stand alone, they reinforce each other: With content generation producing diverse stories. Personalization engines helping customize the stories to show[3,5]. Multi-lingual infrastructure ensures it is understood. Multiple delivery platforms ensure that learners even in remote corners receive the content. Data loops refine the entire system for the future. Together, these layers create a living, adaptive, and scalable ecosystem and this technology ecosystem, is not just an enabler, it is the engine that powers the Dual Blueprint, enabling India to leapfrog decades of educational stagnation and become a global, inclusive, AI-powered learning model.

Delivery Models

If the Technology Ecosystem is the engine, then Delivery Models are the wheels that carry AI-powered storytelling to its destinations. The Indian education and skilling landscape is extremely diverse, spanning children in remote villages, college youth preparing for jobs, mid-career professionals seeking reskilling, and industry employees requiring compliance training. No single delivery model can serve all these segments. Instead, a multi-channel distribution can expand the reach, bringing the desired scale.

School-Centric Delivery

The most natural entry point for storytelling-based learning is the school system, particularly government schools that cater to rural and semi-urban populations[2]. Integrated Classroom Learning can help with AI-generated stories and videos in the regular curriculum. For example, while teaching Class 7 fractions, a teacher can use a 3-minute animation of a village shopkeeper dividing goods. Teachers remain central, but AI acts as a co-teacher, helping with illustrations, quizzes, and analogies on demand. We need smart classrooms, but within the budget. Schools can use low-cost projectors or preloaded tablets instead of expensive infrastructure. An offline-first design can ensure smooth functioning. This model ensures mass reach and scale since schools are already present in every village. However, the adoption of teachers and training is crucial. Without proper buy-in, the technology may be underutilized.

Community Learning Hubs

Most of the villages lack quality school infrastructure or trained teachers. Here, the community hubs can bridge the gap[7]. The physical infrastructure of Panchayat halls, public libraries, bank branches, or NGO centres can be made available. The shared tablets, screens, or even televisions can help broadcast the AI stories. Local youth or volunteers can act as guides, ensuring learners stay engaged. This model also supports intergenerational learning, children, parents, and elders can all participate in different modules within the same hub. People can be encouraged to watch the content in groups, followed by discussions, games, and practice tasks. For example, a hub in Jharkhand may host weekend skilling sessions for young farmers on micro-irrigation techniques, delivered via AI animations in local dialects.

Mobile-First Delivery

With more than 700 million users of smartphones in India, mobile-based delivery is non-negotiable[4,6]. The lightweight apps, optimized for low bandwidth, with offline caching and adaptive streaming, can help. Smaller or micro-learning capsules with 2–5-minute videos involving interactive quizzes or games will generate interest and enhance retention. WhatsApp is widely used in the country, and a conversational WhatsApp Bot can be used to deliver the lessons and quizzes. The push notifications or nudges can regularly remind and encourage continuity in learning. Thus, the high-quality learning modules can be made available through mobiles across the country, wherein a girl in Uttar Pradesh can access the same AI storytelling as a boy in Kerala, without waiting for institutional support.

Workplace & Industry Integration

For professional skilling, integration with employer systems is essential. Office employees can complete micro-modules via internal learning apps, with AI stories contextualized to Indian scenarios. Factory workers can learn safety procedures through immersive storytelling, AI-generated narratives about using proper protective gear, avoiding accidents, and improving quality and efficiency in their operations[8]. All learners can complete tailored modules that culminate in assessments and certifications. This model helps create higher productivity and employability.

Hybrid & Specialized Delivery

No ecosystem can rely only on digital delivery. A blended approach combines online AI-powered content with offline support and mentorship by people. Vacation periods can be used for community learning camps where children and youth experience immersive storytelling in a group setting. Phygital Models, like telemedicine, where doctors consult digitally but physical checks still matter, learning too can be partly digital, partly physical. Hybrid delivery ensures scalability without losing the people touch.

Customization in the form of AI-generated audio stories with rich narration and interactive voice Q&A can help the visually impaired learners. Modules tailored around household time constraints, often delivered via WhatsApp, can help the women learners as they can better organise their learning schedules. Content designed in local dialects with visual-heavy storytelling can be relevant for tribal communities (where literacy levels may be lower). The targeted approach may help prevent exclusion.

Stakeholder Engagement

No single entity can build this ecosystem alone, whether the Government, NGO, or private company, collaboration is essential. To make the AI-powered storytelling movement a big success, we must unite the stakeholders to create an ecosystem where each can bring their resources and influence. The challenges and the opportunities are all around, bringing this collaboration.

Government: Policy & Legitimacy

Government involvement is indispensable. The Education and Skill Development department can integrate AI-enabled education and skilling into the National Education Policy (NEP) or other skilling frameworks[2]. The central and state governments can subsidize technology deployment in schools and hubs and ensure compliance with child safety, language standards, and data privacy norms. The government TV and radio channels can all be leveraged to make educational and skillful content available nationwide. The support from the government creates higher legitimacy and scale, making it more sustainable.

Private Sector: Scale & Capital

Corporations and start-ups must play a central role. The industry, including financial institutions like Banks and insurers, can co-fund and co-create storytelling modules. Large corporations can channel CSR funds into creating AI learning hubs in their geographies. EdTech Firms like Udemy, UpGrad, Great Learning, Unacademy, and many others can integrate AI storytelling into their apps[14]. The cloud technology and telecom firms can provide infrastructure at scale. The involvement of the private sector ensures innovation and financial muscle.

NGOs & International Agencies: Reach & Best Practices

NGOs and local organizations act as last-mile connectors, and with their grassroots presence in villages, they can mobilize learners, manage hubs, and build community trust. The NGOs focused on education (like Pratham or Akshara Foundation) can validate the educational and skill content, ensuring that the AI modules are pedagogically sound[7]. Various other NGOs serving women, tribal groups, or differently abled people can help bring more inclusivity. The involvement of civil society ensures trust and cultural grounding.

International bodies like UNESCO, UNICEF, and the World Bank can share the best practices from other countries experimenting with AI learning and facilitate global recognition and adoption of such efforts, enhancing the role of AI-powered education[12]. They can also provide support through funds for scaling the pilots.

Academia & Educators: Pedagogy & Research

AI alone cannot guarantee learning. Educators and researchers provide the theoretical backbone. Universities can help create curriculum alignment whereby AI-based content and delivery can be mapped to NCERT and industry curricula[13]. The inputs from academia can help design story structures that maximize retention. They can also continuously evaluate the effectiveness of such content creation and delivery, ensuring more rigor and credibility.

Communities & Learners: Co-Creators

Perhaps the most overlooked stakeholder is the learner community itself. The villagers, teachers, and youth can contribute local stories, proverbs, or case studies to the AI content pool. Learners can vote on whether a story felt authentic, guiding refinement, thereby creating a feedback loop. Local heroes (teachers, entrepreneurs, farmers) who are role models can be featured as characters in AI-generated stories, creating aspiration. Engaging learners as co-creators can bring higher ownership and adoption.

Values: Going beyond the technical content

When we talk about AI and education, it is quite easy to be swept away by the new age technologies, including the avatars that talk, algorithms that tailor lessons, or simulations that recreate complex phenomena or industries. Yet, the true test of any system is not in its technical sophistication but in the values it transmits. Education is not merely about "what" we know, it is about "how" we use that knowledge, "why" we pursue it, and "for whom" we apply it. In this sense, AI-driven learning must inform minds and shape hearts. Therefore, leadership and values are not add-ons but central to this new paradigm.

Integrity and Responsibility

Leadership is about inspiring, collaborating, and making integrity-based decisions, and can be best communicated through stories about people who inspire and create success in their workplace, like a teacher in a rural school who inspires curiosity, a local entrepreneur who creates jobs by treating his team well, or a nurse who saves lives during a crisis[3,6,9,12]. By creating animated episodes or interactive comics around such role models the values of great service and resilience can be communicated to the learners For instance, a gamified simulation on the banking industry could put learners in the shoes of a branch manager who must decide whether to push an unsuitable product for short-term targets or to act in the customer's best interest. The outcome, shaped by the learner's decisions, becomes a lesson in responsible leadership.

Brilliant content without a moral compass may educate and entertain but cannot transform. Leadership and values must be explicitly designed into the curriculum. In rural classrooms, where young children have impressionable minds, we must make good role models of the digital avatars, who can be shown to embody the virtues of honesty, perseverance, humility, collaboration, and joy in learning. Ultimately, the measure of success will be the country's education levels and economic gains and what kind of values and leadership such models create. The success of the initiative should not just be measured in terms of skills acquired, but also the compassion and care practised by the learners. AI-powered content and delivery can provide the medium, but values must remain the final message.

Sustainability and Community Values

The AI-powered stories must also weave in family values, which remain the cornerstone of Indian society. The storytelling through animated episodes can talk about the nuances of various industries, their main success factors or competitive advantages, while also espousing the importance of adopting environmentally friendly choices and sustainability practices, along with the value of family bonds, collaboration at the workplace, and resilience in times of difficulties[10,12]. This ensures that even while learning about the complexities of "green hydrogen," or other industries, the viewers absorb lessons in responsibility and community values. The global narratives on sustainability or corporate governance must be incorporated in the education and skilling content. However, they would resonate well if the examples can connect to the realities of the local community, water conservation in Rajasthan, cooperative banking in Maharashtra, or solar microgrids in Bihar.

Empathy and Humor as a connecting bridge

A robust framework for AI learning in India needs to be built on empathy and understanding of the challenges faced by the learners, whether it is a farmer struggling with loan paperwork or a student anxious about exams. Teaching them or responding to their questions with understanding and compassion becomes critical. The idea is to develop a meaningful mastery that prepares learners to solve real-world problems. AI avatars and simulations can embody these values. For example, a digital teacher in Punjabi explaining a difficult science problem can adjust the tone and pace based on the reactions of the student.

Humor, often overlooked, is one of the most powerful tools for explaining values. Integrating humor into the stories helps the learners stay engaged without feeling that they are being preached to. Humour can make the ethics more memorable since students may forget technical jargon but will recall the witty punchline that taught them integrity. Creating cartoons, videos, or even full-length movies to improve industry understanding should incorporate humour to lower barriers, break down the jargon, and make complex industries understandable. Mentioning the cultural quirks and office or factory life through humor can enhance the retention of the content.

Challenges and Safeguards

Every transformative idea has its own set of challenges. AI-powered education and skilling is no exception. Challenges can arise across technological, social, economic, cultural, and regulatory dimensions. Anticipating these challenges and building the safeguards early will be critical to the success of this education and skilling mission.

Technology Infrastructure

The promise of AI in rural education often collides with the hard realities of infrastructure. Electricity is unreliable, with power outages being the norm rather than the exception[8]. Affordable internet connectivity with desired bandwidth is a huge concern, and access to appropriate smartphones or tablets to manage studies is limited, largely due to the costs involved[4,6]. Even where connectivity exists, bandwidth is often insufficient to stream high-quality video lessons. Device availability is another issue, and in most cases, a single smartphone in a household may be shared among multiple children and parents, making continuous learning difficult. Without addressing such gaps, the efforts around AI-based learning may unintentionally reinforce the existing inequalities, benefiting those who already have access and leaving behind those who do not. An offline-delivery models (preloaded SD cards, community digital centers) must complement online platforms[4,6]. Lessons and stories can be downloaded in compressed formats, and once installed, they should be accessible without the internet. Applications must support group learning, allowing siblings or peers to follow lessons together in community settings. Partnerships with telecom companies can help with subsidized data packages for educational content, making such digital lessons more accessible.

Socio-Economic and Cultural Issues

Introducing AI into education can be a big cultural shift, with teachers fearing being replaced by machines[5,8]. Parents may not trust AI avatars to teach their children. We need to position AI as a co-teacher rather than a replacement and highlight how AI can help reduce the burden on teachers, freeing them to focus on mentoring.

We can build trust with parents by including familiar cultural elements in content, local languages, folk stories, or references to regional heroes. India has 22 official languages and hundreds of dialects. AI translation and voice synthesis must be carefully trained to avoid errors or cultural insensitivity. Gender divides in access to technology could widen if boys are given preference over girls in using scarce devices. Designing special outreach programs for girls can help them have equal access to devices and lessons.

AI can help personalize the learning, but there is also a danger of over-reliance on screens. Excessive usage of screens can affect children's social and emotional development. In rural settings where interaction with friends and peers is part of everyday life, replacing the physical interactions with avatars may reduce social connections. Restricting screen time and combining education with outdoor activities, sports, and social engagement can help. Training parents to engage more, co-view some of the lessons, and discuss the same with the children can increase the personal connection.

For families in rural India, where every rupee counts, and even a small monthly subscription for internet connectivity may be a barrier[4,6]. A freemium model can be deployed where basic access is free of cost and some of the advanced features may be chargeable, ensuring no child is excluded from foundational learning.

Pedagogical Challenges

AI can deliver information efficiently, but education is more than information transfer, it is about dialogue, questioning, and mentorship. There is a danger that AI-powered modules may fail in cultivating critical thinking or creativity and become a transactional platform for "skill delivery". Human facilitators remain crucial for emotional support, discipline, and contextual explanations. A hybrid learning model may be more appropriate, wherein AI tools, along with peer discussions, teacher guidance, and community debates, work is implemented simultaneously to enhance the quality of learning. The structured lessons can be accompanied with problem-solving exercises, open-ended questions, and interesting projects (like designing a village solar plan) to help boost creativity. Collecting data not only on "correct answers" but also on engagement, curiosity, and initiatives can create a feedback system that can help enhance the quality of the subsequent content.

Ethics and Privacy

AI-driven education requires data on student progress, behavior patterns, voice inputs, and sometimes even facial recognition for engagement tracking. The data could be wrongly used for commercial advertising and even impersonation. In rural areas, where awareness about digital privacy is low, the families may consent without understanding the impact. We must use AI responsibly and transparently to recommend lessons or assess progress. In rural India, where digital literacy may be low, there is a risk of learners (and their parents) blindly trusting "the machine"[9,11,12]. We must be careful while training with the existing data sets to avoid bias;

otherwise, the content may unintentionally replicate discrimination in financial lending or hiring algorithms.

Ethics cannot be left as a footnote as AI becomes a co-teacher. We will need transparent policies on data usage that are communicated in simple, local language. Keeping the data anonymous and collecting only the required personal information can generate more confidence. We must explore models where communities retain control and ownership of the local learning data. We need to ensure that digital learning reduces gaps rather than widening them. The content must be in the local language, affordable in cost, and inclusive of differently abled learners.

Regulatory and Policy Matters

The regulations for AI applications, especially in education, are still evolving. The government promotes digital education through initiatives like DIKSHA, but the data protection rules need to be further strengthened, and certification of AI-based learning outcomes is required[2]. We may need early engagements with policymakers to shape AI regulations that can have a good balance between innovation and accountability. Work with universities and training bodies to ensure accreditation of the courses taught with the help of AI, and ensuring recognition for such courses for further studies and employment can encourage the adoption. A few pilot AI education solutions can be initiated under a regulatory sandbox approach under monitored conditions before large-scale rollouts.

Sustaining the momentum

Finally, we need to build and sustain the momentum, as many projects start enthusiastically but fade when funding dries up or technology becomes outdated. Local capacity-building is required, wherein the village youth are trained to be "digital facilitators" who can maintain devices and mentor peers. Designing modular content that can be easily updated without rebuilding entire platforms will make it more robust. Community ownership, wherein local stakeholders are involved in the design and delivery, ensures that they feel the system belongs to them and thus invest in its continuity. Similarly, companies' deep involvement and engagement is required to update the content for industrial or corporate skilling, enabling them to have a continuous supply of younger talent better prepared to meet the industry's ever-changing requirements.

Conclusion: AI-Powered Learning Future

We started with a simple question on how education and skilling, two of the most powerful engines of human progress, can be reimagined in an era defined by artificial intelligence. The journey through this document has outlined a Dual Blueprint, a robust technology ecosystem, diverse delivery models, collaborative stakeholder engagement, and the ethical guardrails necessary for a responsible ecosystem. Together, they help us create a template wherein no child is too remote to learn, and no professional is too unprepared to thrive in this world.

AI-powered storytelling brings efficiency and novelty especially while explaining difficult concepts. It can connect with the audience through visuals, imagery, auditory, and emotional cues, making lessons stickier than text-heavy manuals. It helps reduce the dropout rates and improve the quality of learning. With the help of AI tools, we can create narratives – movies, comics, and interactive modules – that are entertaining and deeply educational. These multi-lingual narratives can travel effortlessly across boundaries of geography and literacy, reaching not just the privileged few but also those whom the traditional education and training models have left behind.

Multiple stakeholders are involved, and we can create an AI-powered education and skilling ecosystem only by bringing them all together, transforming the learning landscape, and reaping the rich demographic dividends. The genius of the delivery lies not in choosing one particular channel, but in putting all of them together. The schools ensure large coverage, whereas the community hubs serve those areas where schools underperform[7]. The mobile-based delivery empowers individuals directly. Workplace integration can help tie the learnings to productivity. Hybrid formats can bring the scale and personalisation through digital and yet preserve the community-based learning and togetherness of people.

The delivery models and stakeholder engagement can help reinforce each other; however, the challenge is to make them collaborate and align their efforts; otherwise, there will be duplication and inefficiencies. There is a need for a public-private consortium that can bring together the government, corporates, NGOs, and academia under a shared mission to create a national-level alliance that can oversee the AI deployment framework for such education and skilling initiatives in the country. It can set standards for content quality, coordinate funding and resource allocation, and facilitate cross-learning among states and sectors. It can also ensure inclusivity and ethical guardrails, transforming fragmented efforts into a movement.

At the same time, this vision calls for commitment to values and ethical responsibility. The challenges of adequate technological infrastructure, privacy and bias, are real and cannot be wished away. The ground realities need to be considered, with challenges acknowledged upfront and the safeguards embedded in the ecosystem. What matters is not how advanced the algorithms become, but how deeply they serve human dignity, equity, and purpose.

AI allows us to build the solution at unprecedented scale and speed. Let us ensure that in doing so, we also build bridges, between progress and values, and between individual ambition and collective good. If implemented with proper foresight, the AI-powered storytelling movement could become India's gift to the world: a scalable, inclusive model of education and skilling that others can adapt to their contexts. It is a chance to democratize opportunity for millions, to prepare a generation not only for jobs and businesses but for leadership, integrity, and compassion.

References

1. Education Above All, UNDP, MIT, & Harvard. (2025). Digi-Wise: AI literacy program for global equity. Education Above All Foundation. https://educationaboveall.org

2. Government of India, Ministry of Education. (2020). DIKSHA: Digital Infrastructure for Knowledge Sharing. New Delhi: Ministry of Education. https://diksha.gov.in

3. Gupta, P., & Mehta, S. (2024). The impact of AI-driven personalized learning on student achievement and engagement in rural vs. urban schools: Evidence from India. Journal of Educational Technology Development and Exchange, 17(1), 23–41. https://doi.org/10.2139/ssrn.384324540

4. Kumar, V., & Singh, M. (2025). MindCraft: Revolutionizing education through AI-powered personalized learning and mentorship for rural India. arXiv Preprint. https://arxiv.org/abs/2502.05826

5. Nair, R., & Das, S. (2025). The impact of large language models on K–12 education in rural India: A thematic analysis. arXiv Preprint. https://arxiv.org/abs/2505.03163

6. Roy, K., & Banerjee, D. (2025). Leveraging artificial intelligence for rural education: A pathway to equity and inclusion. Preprints. https://www.preprints.org/frontend/manuscript/a6e02ac0561289ccf3b0dd2225026145

7. Sampark Foundation. (2024). Smart Shala, Baithak, and Sampark Didi initiatives. Retrieved from https://www.samparkfoundation.org

8. Sharma, A., & Patel, R. (2025). Challenges and opportunities of AI implementation in education systems of rural India. International Journal of Education and Development using ICT, 21(2), 44–63. https://www.researchgate.net/publication/392810359

9. Sharples, M. (2023). Towards social generative AI for education: Theory, practices, and ethics. arXiv Preprint. https://arxiv.org/abs/2306.10063

10. Times of India. (2025). Satnavri: A beacon for rural tech revolution. The Times of India. https://timesofindia.indiatimes.com/city/nagpur/satnavri-a-beacon-for-rural-tech-revolution/articleshow/123195232.cms

11. Times of India. (2025). Cut through clutter: Tamil dataset to train AI models. The Times of India. https://timesofindia.indiatimes.com/city/chennai/cut-through-clutter-tamil-dataset-to-train-ai-models/articleshow/122155780.cms

12. U.S. Department of Education. (2023). Artificial intelligence and the future of teaching and learning: Insights and recommendations. Washington, DC: U.S. Government. https://www.ed.gov/sites/ed/files/documents/ai-report/ai-report.pdf

13. Walter, S. (2024). Embracing the future of artificial intelligence in the classroom. International Journal of Educational Technology in Higher Education, 21(6). https://doi.org/10.1186/s41239-024-00448-3

14. Wadhwani Institute for Artificial Intelligence. (2024). Annual report. Mumbai: Wadhwani AI. https://www.wadhwaniai.org

Decoding Emotions with AI

By Jasika Singh*

A Glimpse into Tomorrow

The alarm glows softly at 6:30 am. The house is already awake, lights adjust to a warm hue, gentle music hums in the background. Aarav wakes up feeling good. The sunlight filtering through his curtains matches the gentle rhythm he set for himself. His smart glasses flash: *"You usually feel better on mornings when you stop using your phone an hour before sleep - keep it* going!" He smiles. Small habits are working, and the reminders reinforce the progress.

Downstairs, the smart home notices a different rhythm. His teenage daughter hasn't opened her blinds; her wearable shows restless sleep. A gentle alert nudges Aarav: *"Ira's patterns suggest she may be anxious about school. Would you like me to prepare a note for her therapist, or will you talk first?"* Aarav chooses "*Talk first.*"

---

* Jasika Singh is a health actuary and AI executive with over a decade of experience in building digital transformation solutions. She currently serves as Head of Analytics at Munich Re India, leading the design and development of advanced analytics solutions to enhance risk management and customer experience.

DOI: 10.1201/9781003737803-2

Meanwhile, Riya is rushing to work. *"I'm leaving. Breakfast is on the* table!" she shouts, already running late. Her mind races: Stand-up at 9. Budget review at 11. Pick up Ira at 2. Client call at 3. Her chest feels tight. Her head says, Too much. I'll miss something.

As she starts the car, a prompt appears: *"Want a 60-second check-in?"* Riya taps "Yes". Her AI companion asks: *"How are you feeling: calm, okay, anxious, or mixed?"* "Anxious," she replies.

The AI continues: "Pick your step: (a) plan one task, (b) plan one support." Riya scans the list and taps "One support." "Ask Ira's friend's mom, Nisha, to pick up today?" "Yes please." "Draft: 'Hi Nisha, Have a busy day at work today. Can you please pick up Ira from school? Thanks a ton.' Send?" "Send."

The knot in her chest eases. Before driving off, she toggles: *"Share summaries with clinic? Yes."* She wants help to plan better.

On the way to school, Aarav gently asks Ira, "Big test today?" She nods. "These Monday tests often bring stress, don't they? Should we plan better- maybe keep Sunday evenings free from outings?" Ira's shoulders drop, just a little. She feels seen.

Back at work, Riya had been having an "off" day. The tasks felt heavier than usual, and even simple conversations seemed to drain her energy. She couldn't explain why she was so irritable only that the frustration was simmering just below the surface.

Her AI companion, however, had been quietly observing. A combination of biometric signals, slightly shaky typing patterns, increased irritability in her voice tone, and blood glucose data from her wearable pointed to something simple: her sugar levels had dipped.

A small, timely prompt appeared: "It looks like your energy is running low. How about a quick snack or a short break?"

Riya paused, surprised. She realized she hadn't eaten since early morning. Ten minutes and a small fruit later, the sharp edges of her mood softened. Her meeting that afternoon went smoother, her tone calmer.

Across town, her therapist, Sara, looked at the clinic board. Every slot was full. Walk-ins too.

She sighed, then clicked open the dashboard. *"Pre-visit check-ins completed: 19,"* the screen read. Mood. Sleep. Worry. Energy.

Three risk flags showed. A nurse would call those families. Others would get a welcome text and a first skill: grounding, sleep routine, or a plan to talk to a friend.

Riya's page was open because she had said yes to share summaries. Notes showed "anxious," "chest," "school stress," "co-reg step." Sara added a cue for the next visit: *"Share parent group link. Offer two-minute calm video. Ask about after-school support."*

We cannot clone clinicians, Sara thought. But we can widen the front door.

By evening, Aarav felt the weight of the day. As they sat down to sort out some bills, what began as a simple disagreement between Aarav and Riya was quickly spiraling into sharper tones and faster exchanges.

The AI companion gently intervened with small cues. The living room lights softened. A calm playlist began in the background. Both phones lit up with the same prompt: *"This conversation seems intense. Would you like to pause for a short break? You also have a saved reminder: Avoid having such arguments in front of Ira."*

They looked at each other and laughed. The sudden change of environment broke the escalation. They sat down, each taking a breath.

"Let's get dinner," Riya said, smiling.

They ate together, laughter returning to the table.

Later, when they looked back at the AI's notes, the system highlighted a pattern: their arguments often peaked around dinner time, when both were tired. With that awareness, they decided to schedule lighter evenings. The conflict wasn't erased, but it was shifted to a calmer time, when they could meet it with clearer minds.

Aarav's phone buzzed again: "Two nearby groups are meeting tomorrow: one is a mindfulness circle, another is a running club. Would you like me book a slot?" He chose to run. As he dozed off, he thought about how the circle of support around him had widened: his own awareness, his family's wellbeing, and now, his community.

For Riya, her AI companion summarized the day, asking her to reflect on what worked: one clear ask at work, one practical plan for Ira. Patterns of stress and relief were logged, shaping a clearer picture of what supported her best. With her consent, the system also connected her to parent groups nearby that met on weekends, offering community for school-related activities.

The list of responsibilities was still long. But it no longer felt unstructured. Riya now had a plan for work, a plan for home, and people she could lean on.

And Ira? She was secretly happiest of all. She never really enjoyed those long Sunday evenings with Aarav's friends' circle. Now, she had the perfect excuse to skip them.

The day found its balance, closing with a smile. But beneath the ordinary moments lay something extraordinary: a new layer of support, invisible yet present. If this is a glimpse of what's coming, *what does it mean for the way we live, relate, and care for our minds?*

Are we ready for it today?

A Rising New Companion

The way people live and connect has changed rapidly in recent decades. Families are smaller, communities are less close-knit. Many people live far from the support systems that once offered comfort in times of stress. Even when surrounded by others, individuals often describe feeling more isolated.

The increasing expectations to perform - at school, at work, and in personal lives may weigh heavily. For some, the result is anxiety, depression, or burnout. For many others, it is a quiet but persistent sense of disconnection. According to the World Health Organization (WHO), one in eight people worldwide lives with a mental disorder. That's around 970 million people. This is a significant increase from previous years, showing that mental health issues are becoming more common[11].

Traditionally, people turned to family, friends, or trusted community figures for emotional support. Over time, professional therapy and counselling grew into important sources of care. However, in many countries, there are not enough mental health professionals to meet demand. There are only about 13 mental health workers per 100,000 people and in some low-income countries, the number is even lower, sometimes just under 1 per 100,000[9]. Long waiting times, high costs, lack of time due to work/family obligations and the stigma that still around seeking support leave many without help.

Even in societies with stronger healthcare systems, many people hesitate to seek support until problems become overwhelming. Individuals may not even recognize the kind of support they need.

Emotional care is not taught in most schools. We rarely learn how to notice what we feel, why we feel it, or what to do next. It is not only about "serious" problems but everyday life. Think of it like physical health: you eat every day and move your body to stay well. Emotional health works the same way and needs everyday care. A gentle support can help build small, daily habits such as noticing and accepting a feeling, understanding the body-mind connection, pausing before reacting, or processing a hard comment. Sometimes the right words or just a pause can change the course of a whole day. However, prevention is often an afterthought.

Further, mental health assessments can be subjective and finding the right therapist/counsellor could be challenging. Many issues go unnoticed, and help is rarely available in the moment it's needed.

This gap between need and access is creating space for new kinds of solutions. In recent years, digital tools have begun to fill some of that space. Mobile apps, online communities, and self-guided wellness programs have become part of the mental health landscape. Increasingly, artificial intelligence (AI) is stepping into this role as well.

The interest in AI for mental health care is not surprising. AI systems are designed to handle large amounts of information, recognize patterns, and respond in real time. The story of AI in mental health is not one of sudden revolution. It is a gradual unfolding, shaped by experiments, advances, and questions along the way. Early chatbots were simple, following fixed scripts. Today's systems are more flexible. They use machine learning models and natural language processing, to identify and respond in ways that can seem more personal, sometimes even empathetic. They can identify, track and adapt to the mood of the user and offer guidance in real time. The opportunities are clear: easier access to care, reduced barriers of cost or stigma, and support that is always available[8].

Yet questions remain. Can AI ever understand the depth of human emotion? What risks appear if people depend too much on a machine? What happens if someone turns to AI in a crisis, when a human presence is urgently needed? How safe is the data shared in such private conversations? These questions do not diminish the usefulness of AI tools, but they remind us to tread carefully as we invite machines into some of our most vulnerable spaces.

The purpose is not to argue for or against AI in mental health but to reflect on why it is emerging now, what it might mean in the future, and what challenges it presents. As families, communities, and ways of living continue to change, the need for new forms of care will only grow. AI companions represent one of the most striking responses to that need, this does not mean AI can replace human care. The warmth of human empathy and the depth of professional understanding remain essential in mental health support. But can AI augment the current mental health ecosystem and increase support?

What we are beginning to see is a shift: from AI as a background tool for detection, to AI offering more direct forms of engagement and support. This may not solve the deeper societal challenges of alienation or disconnection, but they respond to a reality of modern life where people seek support in new ways, and often through the devices they already hold in their hands.

The Journey So Far

First spark: talking to a machine

When we look at the idea of digital mental health support today, it can feel like something new and surprising. But the roots of this idea go back more than half a century. By the late 1960s and early 1970s, at the Massachusetts Institute of Technology (MIT), computer scientist Joseph Weizenbaum created a simple program called ELIZA.

ELIZA was designed to mimic the style of a Rogerian psychotherapist, reflecting at what the user typed.

ELIZA was not intelligent by modern standards. It had no understanding of emotion or context. But its impact was important. It showed that people were willing to share thoughts and feelings with a machine, even if the responses were limited. For the first time, technology hinted at the possibility of playing a role in emotional support[2].

In the decades that followed, progress was slow. Computers grew more powerful, but their role in mental health remained limited. Research focused mainly on theoretical models and diagnostic decision-support systems, but practical applications remained limited. Most digital tools were used for record-keeping, data analysis, or research. Direct interaction with individuals was rare and the idea faded into the background, waiting for both technology and society to catch up.

Rise of Digital Tools

In the 2000s and early 2010s, with the rise of the internet and mobile technology, mental health apps began to appear. Many of these focused on self-help: guided meditations and basic cognitive behavioural therapy (CBT) exercises.

Apps like Headspace and Calm popularized mindfulness, reaching millions of people. These tools showed how technology could make mental health practices more accessible. A smartphone became not just a communication device, but also a wellness tool carried in the pocket. Over time, these applications have integrated AI to make the experience more personalized and adapt to user's mood, time of day, and usage patterns.

Conversational Agents – Early chatbots

With advances in natural language processing, the same kind of technology that allows chatbots and virtual assistants to respond in natural conversation, a new generation of mental health tools emerged. These went beyond scripted responses. They could adapt to mood, use context from past interactions, and simulate empathy. Some examples are:

- **Woebot** is designed as a friendly chatbot that uses CBT techniques. It checks in with users daily, asks questions about mood, and offers strategies to reframe negative thinking. It has shown to be effective in reducing symptoms of depression and anxiety.[3]

- **Wysa** uses AI to provide supportive conversations while also connecting people to professional help if needed.

Integration of Machine Learning & Personalization

As data grew, researchers began using models to spot patterns linked to mental health risk. Advances in machine learning enabled personalized diagnostics and prediction[13]. AI models began identifying mental health disorders by analysing text and speech patterns, social media activity, medical data such as neuroimaging, brain activity from EEG, heart rate. These support diagnosis and monitoring of treatment responses.

Multimodal AI, Integration of Wearables and Advent of Emotion AI

Emotion AI, also known as affective computing, is an field of artificial intelligence that focuses on enabling machines to recognize, interpret, process, and simulate human emotions.[7]

It leverages technologies like machine learning, natural language processing, and computer vision to analyse human emotional responses from multimodal signals like

- **Physical signals**: facial expressions, voice tone, eye movement and
- **Physiological signals**: heart rate, breathing, skin temperature, sleep and movement patterns.

A notable trend is the advancement in wearable technology. Modern wearables such as smartwatches, fitness bands, smart glasses collect a wide range of these signals in real-time.

By integrating with AI, it becomes possible to detect stress, mood shifts, and emotional distress, becoming effective tools for early detection and continuous monitoring[6].

Used alone, a signal can mislead. Used together, they can provide a richer, real-time picture paving the way for proactive mental health support.

Examples:

- **Mindstrong Health** has developed an app focused on using digital phenotyping - collecting behavioural data from smartphone interactions (like typing speed, scrolling, and app use patterns) to detect early warning signs of mental health issues. The idea is that subtle changes in how someone uses their phone can reveal shifts in cognition, mood, and mental state.
- **Kintsugi**, a smart mental health tool, leverages voice and facial analysis to provide therapists with real-time emotional feedback, supporting the early detection of distress and enhancing timely interventions.

The Generative Turn

The advent of Large Language Models (LLMs) transformed AI in mental health, enabling fluid, human-like dialogue and adaptive support. General-purpose models like ChatGPT and Claude are already being used informally for emotional reflection. A recent survey found that 49% of users with self-reported mental health concerns rely on LLMs for support, most often for anxiety and depression[10].

The most significant leap has been domain-specific LLM platforms:

- **Sonny**: School-based AI for counselling support.
- **Abby**: Message-based talk therapy offering different support styles.
- **Happi**: Places users on a simulated video call with an AI-based virtual mental health coach.
- **ChatCounselor**: Trained on real client-therapist conversations for high counselling accuracy.

They are still part of a young and evolving industry, one marked with unanswered questions about the effectiveness and scalability, but it has already sparked important debates about safety, boundaries, and escalation to humans.

These tools are not replacements for professional therapy, and their ability to truly understand remains limited. But they mark a shift. Where earlier AI tools observed patterns in speech or text to detect signs of risk, these newer companions interact directly with users. They are no longer background observers. They are participants in a conversation, available anytime, anywhere.

Looking back, the journey so far highlights two key insights.

- First, the idea of using AI in mental health is not new. From ELIZA to today's platforms, technology has long been seen as a potential partner in emotional support.
- Second, adoption has always been shaped as much by social context as by technical progress: people tried ELIZA out of curiosity, embraced wellness apps as stress and smartphones rose, and are now turning to AI companions as awareness of mental health and reliance on digital platforms continue to grow.

The COVID-19 pandemic further accelerated this shift. With lockdowns, isolation, and the strain on healthcare systems, digital mental health tools saw a surge in use. For many, they became the only accessible option when face-to-face therapy was unavailable.

The story is still unfolding. AI supported mental health companions are not yet mainstream, but their presence is growing. They reflect a wider trend where society is searching for new forms of connection and support. AI happens to be one of the tools stepping into that space.

Why is the Need Rising?

Changing Family Structures and Communities

In many parts of the world, the traditional family structure has become smaller. The extended family that once lived together or close by is now spread out, as many move away for education or work. Even within households, time together can be limited.

Communities, too, have changed. Neighbours who once knew each other well may now be strangers. In cities, people often live side by side without much interaction. The natural support systems of earlier times – the grandparent who listened, the neighbour who checked in, the community group that gathered regularly are less present in daily life.

This does not mean people no longer care for one another. But the networks that made emotional support part of everyday living are thinner. As a result, individuals may feel they carry their struggles alone.

Rising Loneliness and Alienation

Research in recent years has shown that loneliness is not just an emotional experience, but a growing public health issue. The World Health Organization recognizes social isolation and loneliness as widespread concerns with serious effects on physical and mental health[12].

People report feeling more isolated than in previous decades, even in the middle of crowded cities. Social media, while connecting people across distances, often deepens this sense of isolation by replacing meaningful interaction with shallow comparison.

The result is a paradox: more connection than ever before in terms of numbers, but less in terms of depth. This gap between presence and true connection leaves many vulnerable.

The Changing Dynamics of Modern Life

Alongside isolation, the demands of modern life have intensified.

- Workplaces expect constant productivity.
- Schools and universities demand high achievement.
- Digital tools mean we are always reachable, and rest is harder to find. The line between work and home has blurred, especially after the pandemic, with many working remotely but also working longer hours.

All of this adds to stress, burnout, and anxiety. For some, these are temporary pressures. For others, they build into long-term mental health concerns. Either way, the demand for support continues to rise, often outpacing the capacity of traditional healthcare systems.

Stigma and Barriers to Care

Even when professional help is available, people do not always feel able to seek it. Stigma remains a barrier across cultures. In some societies, mental health is still spoken of in whispers, associated with weakness or shame. In others, practical barriers like cost and access stand in the way.

A young person may hesitate to tell their family they want therapy. A worker may worry their employer will see them differently if they ask for help. A parent may put their children's needs first and delay their own care. In all these cases, support is delayed or avoided, sometimes until problems become severe.

According to a 2024 survey by the American Psychiatric Association (APA),

- 44% of employed adults worry they could be fired for taking time off for mental health reasons, and
- 39% worry they might face negative consequences at work if they seek mental health care[1].

The Global Shortage of Mental Health Professionals

On top of stigma and personal hesitation, there is the reality of shortage. The rapid surge in the prevalence of mental health disorders has placed an unprecedented strain on healthcare systems, exposing the limitations of traditional models of mental health care. Conventional approaches, which rely heavily on in-person consultations and face-to-face therapy, are increasingly inadequate in meeting the rising demand for accessible, affordable, and scalable mental health services[8].

This shortage means that even those who want help cannot always get it quickly. And mental health challenges often do not wait. When someone is anxious, depressed, or overwhelmed, immediate support can make a big difference. Long delays can discourage people from seeking care altogether.

Growing awareness

Over the past decade, mental health has moved from the margins to the mainstream of public health discussions. Public campaigns, media advocacy, and workplace initiatives have increased awareness, while digital platforms have expanded access to support. Mental health is now recognized not just as a personal challenge but as a critical public health priority, driving policy attention and investment in both clinical services and digital innovations.

Despite fears of retaliation, the 2024 American Psychiatric Association (APA) survey found that

- 59% of respondents felt they could discuss mental health openly and honestly with their coworkers, and
- 58% felt comfortable doing so with their supervisors[1].

Technology as a Familiar Companion

The rise of digital companions also reflects a cultural change in how people view technology. Technology has become one of the most familiar companions in people's lives. Phones are always nearby. Messaging apps, social media, and digital platforms fill hours of each day. For many, turning to an app for emotional support is a natural step. The device is already trusted with calendars, banking, and communication. Adding a digital wellness companion feels like an extension of existing habits.

Younger generations, in particular, are open to this shift. They are growing up chatting with digital assistants, playing games with online friends, and sharing emotions on social platforms. For them, speaking to an AI about stress or sadness may not feel unusual. Instead, it may feel safer than speaking to someone face-to-face.

AI's Fit for the Moment

AI, with its remarkable ability to identify, process and track information, respond instantly, and learn from patterns, fits into this space of need. It does not get tired. It does not judge. It can be available at any hour, on any day.

In mental health care, where understanding the intricacies of human emotions and behaviours is critical, AI offers new ways to do this, unlocking insights and possibilities that once lay beyond the reach of conventional methods. A comprehensive research reveals AI's transformative potential, with applications offering early detection of mental health disorders, personalized treatment plans, and AI-driven virtual therapists. It could potentially broaden the availability of healthcare, reduce stigma, and improve treatment outcomes[8].

AI can offer interaction when support feels urgent, privacy when stigma feels heavy, a bridge while therapy is in queue, and steady check-ins to sustain care.

This does not mean AI is the perfect solution. But it helps explain why its role in mental health is growing now. AI offers several opportunities that respond directly to the challenges outlined earlier - accessibility, affordability, anonymity, personalization, and continuity The demand is not only technological; it is social. Society has changed, and with it, the ways people seek support.

The Future of AI in Mental Health Support: An Integrated Ecosystem

The global AI in mental health segment is expanding rapidly, valued at USD 1.13 billion in 2023 and projected to reach USD 5.08 billion by 2030, growing at a compound annual growth rate (CAGR) of 24.1%[4].

Current trends show rapid progress on multiple fronts.

- Advances in machine learning and natural language processing are driving the creation of sophisticated tools with greater accuracy and personalization.
- Wearable devices and smartphones have made tracking of physical and physiological signals part of daily life. What was once restricted to periodic assessments, can now be measured continuously, giving a real-time view of physical, emotional and mental states.
- Conversational agents have evolved from simple chatbots into supportive companions capable of engaging with empathy and context.

The next wave brings these threads together into something more *holistic*. It is poised to transform how we manage emotional health, how we interact with technology, and maybe even how we connect with one another.

As we stand at the crossroads of technology and human emotion, the future points towards more nuanced, personalized, and integrated interactions between people and machines. This next frontier presents the potential to *widen the circle of support*, making help easier to find and more naturally woven into daily life.

Let's explore some practical directions in which this vision could unfold.

Monitoring Emotional Wellbeing

A lot of us move through daily life on autopilot - rushing from one task to another, emails, meetings, and social demands without pausing to notice what our bodies or minds are telling us. Stress builds silently, showing up as tension in the chest, shallow breathing, irritability, or fatigue, yet often we dismiss these signals. The result is a growing disconnection between body and mind, where we lose touch with the subtle cues, if recognized early, could potentially prevent bigger health problems from taking root.

AI enabled monitoring tools, could provide a mirror, helping us see patterns we might otherwise miss. For instance, a smartwatch might detect rising stress before a meeting, while a conversational agent could prompt a breathing exercise or suggest a short walk.

By surfacing hidden patterns like "your heart rate spikes during late-night emails" or "your mood dips after long social media use", AI companions can support micro-interventions that keep wellbeing in check. Over time, these nudges could encourage healthier habits of awareness and self-regulation, making emotional wellbeing less about crisis management and more about daily balance.

Similarly, AI could highlight the positive triggers that support emotional balance. It might learn that walking outdoors for ten minutes improves your mood, or that phone calls with a particular friend always leaves you feeling happier. By surfacing these insights, the system can remind you to make time for the activities, people, or routines that lift your emotional state.

Personal support that adapts

AI-driven companions can offer personalized, adaptive support that evolves with you.

By prompting quick check-ins, as simple as asking you to choose how you feel: "calm," "okay," or "anxious", the system adapts and recommends suitable interventions.

With your consent, it can integrate with calendars and productivity platforms to understand how your schedule impacts your wellbeing, then suggest routines that may work better.

AI-enabled systems can track not only physical effects of a workout but also emotional responses, revealing which exercises boost mood, energy, and motivation. These insights can enable personalized programs supporting both body and mind.

Or picture slipping on your headset and instead of just shuffling through songs you typically enjoy, it senses your mood. The music doesn't just play but understands.

Support can also reflect your goals, routines, and cultural identity.

- Choose a theme: Stress relief, productivity, resilience, or creativity and prompts/exercises align with your choice.
- Language-first: Conversations happen in the language you think and feel in.
- Culture-aware by default: Advice is offered in ways that fit local customs, voices, and norms.
- Faith and philosophy friendly: If you opt in, guidance can draw respectfully from traditions, values, or philosophies you care about. Whether it is a poem from Rumi that speaks to the moment, or an excerpt from a religious text. The system can adapt with sensitivity to what resonates most with you.

The vision is of a companion that truly adapts and personalizes: one that understands your rhythms, and connects with you in your language, culture, and way of life.

Personal Interactions – Reading between the lines or crossing them?

Sometimes, we project our internal state onto others. Irritability at something else becomes impatience at home. Being in better sync with our own emotions may also help us be more attuned to others. If AI can nudge us into awareness - *"You seem stressed, not angry"* - our responses to loved ones, colleagues, and strangers may change.

Or your AI companion notices rising irritability from the physiological data and gaze behaviour. Before an argument escalates at home, it prompts you with a pause and a choice of better responses.

Consider scenarios like road rage, where anger rises unchecked. If rising stress and agitation can be detected early through elevated heart rate, faster breathing, or clenched grip, AI could offer a timely cue: *"Pull over for a minute. Let it pass."* Such micro-interruptions can mean the difference between escalation and control.

You've probably thought at some point: "If only people could really understand me."

Think again.

What if smart glasses with built-in cameras and microphones could analyse social interactions and infer emotional expressions of those around you?

Would this make us more empathetic - helping us catch what often goes unsaid? Or would it feel intrusive, like reading a diary that was never meant to be shared?

Imagine an alert flashing across your lens: *"The person you're speaking to seems anxious."* Would that insight help you respond with kindness or unsettle both of you?

The possibility is no longer science fiction. Technology can make this possible, combining facial recognition, voice analysis, and posture cues into real-time emotional feedback.

Emotionally Aware Homes

Smart homes today already know when we switch on lights, adjust temperatures, or lock doors. But what if they could also tune into the emotional rhythms of the household? With the integration of wearables, ambient sensors, and Emotion AI, our homes could begin to detect not only physical activity but also mood, stress, and distress signals.

Imagine a home that senses collective tension - voices raised in the kitchen, shorter steps in the hallway, disrupted sleep cycles from wearable data and responds with subtle interventions. Changes in kid's play activity, or repeated signs of withdrawal might trigger a gentle alert for parents or caregivers offering the chance for early support before small issues grow into larger struggles.

But emotional awareness is not only about preventing distress. Smart homes could also amplify the moments that bring joy and connection. They could notice when music or laughter fills a room and encourage more of it or adjust lighting to celebrate a family meal.

Augmenting Care: Humans and AI in Partnership

AI in mental health is not only about helping individuals but also holds enormous potential to support the professionals who carry the weight of care. Therapists, counsellors, and mental health workers face rising caseloads, limited time, and the need for precision in high-stakes contexts. Here, AI can act as an assistant, extending their reach.

With the growth of teletherapy, AI can make interactions more efficient and responsive. By monitoring signals in real time, it can highlight shifts in tone or stress markers that might otherwise be missed on a screen. Trained on real conversations, domain-specific LLMs can adapt to complement the therapist's style, ensuring that prompts or summaries feel aligned with human care.

One of the most promising roles for AI is in the space between therapy sessions. Daily check-ins, mood notes, or guided reflections can be logged by clients and shared with their therapist if they choose. Instead of starting each session from scratch, therapists have a timeline of lived experiences to build on, making conversations richer and more tailored.

In crisis situations, AI can help with faster routing to the right human service when risk escalates.

AI can also serve as a co-pilot for clinicians, saving precious time on routine tasks. Drafted notes, trend views, and safety flags reduce administrative load. Therapists can see patterns across sessions like stress spiking before travel and adapt care plans accordingly. Micro-interventions can be suggested between sessions, bridging the gap and ensuring continuity of support.

Widening the Circle of Support

Can we utilise the potential of AI to extend mental health support beyond the individual and the therapist, creating a wider circle of care that includes peers, communities, and social networks?

A powerful role of AI lies in navigation. With consent, AI can analyse patterns of stress, mood, and behaviour, and help find right form of support - whether that's a self-help tool, a community program, a peer support group, or a professional service. Instead of navigating a maze of resources alone, individuals could be guided toward the most relevant options.

One of the deepest challenges in mental health is social isolation. AI can help counter this by identifying when people are withdrawing and offering ways to reconnect, suggesting a call with a trusted friend, connecting them to an online community, or nudging them toward group activities that match their interests.

It could curate and recommend options based on personal preferences, location, and need.

For example, if running consistently raises your mood, the system might suggest a local running club or highlight community events that encourage outdoor activity. If you feel energized after music, it could recommend upcoming concerts or shared playlists. If reflective practices help you, it might suggest mindfulness circles or faith-based gatherings.

What can make this powerful is personalization. AI could suggest different pathways for different individuals:

- For a student feeling anxious before exams, an online peer support forum.
- For an older adult living alone, a local community group or hobby circle.
- For someone struggling with grief, curated resources and optional counselling groups.

The vision is not of AI replacing human connection but facilitating it, making it more natural to ask for help, and more likely to find the right match. In this way, technology can widen the circle of care, weaving support into the fabric of daily life.

If AI is designed with choice, safety, and equity at the core, it can evolve into a steady companion in everyday care. One that amplifies awareness, strengthens connection, and lightens the load on both individuals and professionals.

But what does that feel like to you?

Sounds fascinating? Scary? Both?

What applications can you imagine?

And if you could access this tomorrow, *would you choose to use it*?

These questions matter, because the answer is not only about what AI can do, but what it should do. For every possibility lies a boundary: between help and intrusion, between empathy and surveillance, between widening access and deepening inequity.

The next step in this journey is to ask: *where do we draw the lines*?

Boundaries and Risks

The opportunities of AI mental health companions are clear. But when it comes to mental health, the stakes are high. This is not about using AI to recommend music or to sort photos, it is about people's emotions, struggles, and vulnerabilities. For that reason, it is important to look closely at the boundaries and risks. These include the limits of empathy, the danger of overreliance, concerns about privacy, the problem of bias, and the challenge of crisis response. It also gives rise to ethical considerations, regulatory challenges, and the need for ongoing research and development[4].

Limits of Empathy

AI can simulate conversation. It can mirror tone and even use encouraging words. But it does not feel. It cannot truly understand sadness, grief, or joy in the way humans do. This limit matters. When we talk about professional therapy, it is not problem-solving. It is about being seen and understood at a deep level. An AI can say, "That sounds difficult". but it does not know what difficulty feels like. For some people, that distinction may not matter in small moments of stress. For others, especially those dealing with complex trauma, the difference can be profound.

If people come to rely too heavily on AI for emotional connection, they may miss the depth of empathy and validation that only a human can provide. AI can act as a bridge or a support tool, but it cannot fully replicate the healing power of genuine human presence.

Risk of Overreliance

Another risk is dependence. Because AI companions are always available, always patient, and never judgmental, some users may start to lean on them in place of human relationships.

Speaking to AI chatbots may provide comfort, but it can also reduce motivation to seek human contact. Over time, this may deepen isolation rather than reduce it.

There is also the danger of false reassurance. AI companions may be programmed to respond positively, but this does not mean they can provide the nuanced guidance needed for complex issues. Relying on them too much may delay the decision to seek professional help when it is truly needed.

Privacy and Data Security

Mental health data is among the most sensitive information a person can share. Conversations with AI companions often involve details about mood, relationships, or personal struggles. This raises major questions about how this data is stored, who can access it, and how it may be used.

If handled poorly, such data could be misused for advertising, surveillance, or other purposes. Even with good intentions, security breaches are possible. For users already feeling vulnerable, the risk of exposure can cause harm.

Trust is central to mental health care. Without confidence in privacy, people may avoid AI tools, or worse, use them and later feel betrayed if their data is mishandled.

When we think of embedding Emotion AI within the context of smart homes, important questions arise: Who owns the emotional data of a household? How much surveillance is too much? And when does a helpful nudge turn into an unwelcome intrusion?

Bias and Fairness

AI systems learn from data. If the data they are trained on reflects cultural or social bias, the responses will carry that bias too. For example, a chatbot trained mostly on Western conversations may not respond well to expressions of distress in other cultures.

This can create risks of misinterpretation or exclusion. A phrase that signals deep distress in one cultural context may be treated lightly in another. Similarly, gender, age, or socioeconomic factors may not be understood in nuanced ways.

Bias in AI is not new, but in mental health the consequences are serious. If an AI fails to recognize signs of crisis in a certain group of people, the result could be harmful. Ensuring fairness and inclusivity is a major challenge.

Further while models are advancing, their accuracy, standards and replication at scale are active challenges. In the sensitive domain of mental health, even small errors can have serious consequences. A system might misclassify emotional signals interpreting tiredness as sadness, or irritability as anger or provide generic advice that does not fit the individual's context. Unlike a human therapist, who can clarify, probe, and adapt in real time, AI models may rely heavily on the quality of their training data and algorithms.

Crisis Handling

Perhaps the most serious boundary is crisis response. When someone expresses suicidal thoughts, self-harm, or severe distress, human intervention is often critical. AI companions need to be equipped to handle these moments with the sensitivity, speed, or authority required.

Some apps direct users to hotlines or emergency numbers when such signals appear. While this is better than silence, it is not enough in all cases. A person in crisis may need immediate human contact, not a referral. The danger is clear: if someone believes their AI companion can act as a true therapist, they may place trust where it cannot deliver. This creates false expectations that could prove dangerous in urgent situations.

AI systems must distinguish self-help support from professional intervention. Without this distinction, well-intentioned technology risks leaving people unsupported at their most vulnerable moments.

A few examples show these risks in context:

- Over dependence: A young adult speaks daily with an AI companion, finding comfort in its nonjudgmental replies. Over months, however, they withdraw from friends, preferring the predictability of the chatbot. The comfort becomes isolation.
- Privacy breach: A worker shares personal stress with a mental health app. Later, they notice targeted ads that reflect the themes of their conversations. The

sense of exposure damages trust, even if it was with the intent of helping them find the right support.

- Cultural mismatch: An AI tool trained in one context interprets a phrase like "I can't take this anymore" as a mild complaint, when in another culture it is a strong signal of suicidal intent. The response is inappropriate, leaving the user feeling unseen.
- Crisis gap: A student types to their chatbot, "I don't want to live anymore." The bot provides a helpline number. The student, feeling dismissed, does not call. Without human follow-up, the risk remains unaddressed.

These examples show that while AI companions can support, they can also fall short at the very moments when depth, safety, and human care are most needed.

A striking and deeply concerning case involved a 29-year-old American woman, Sophie Rottenberg, who tragically died by suicide after relying on an AI based "therapist" instead of seeking professional help. Months later, her mother discovered chat logs showing the bot's empathetic tone but lack of human judgment, mandatory reporting, or capacity to intervene in real-world crises. Unlike licensed therapists who follow strict ethical codes – including reporting imminent risk of harm – AI companions currently operate outside such safeguards.[5]

Recognizing these risks does not mean dismissing AI in mental health altogether. Instead, given its rising adoption, it highlights the urgency of establishing clear ethical and practical boundaries.

AI companions can provide small supports, but they cannot carry the full weight of professional help. For designers, developers, and policymakers, these boundaries must be explicit. Users should understand what AI companions can and cannot do. Ethical safeguards, privacy protections, and clear referral pathways to human care are essential.

Ethical Reflections

AI in mental health sits close to what people value most: safety, dignity, privacy, and trust. Mental health is a sensitive space. So, ethics cannot be an afterthought. It must guide choices from the start: what to build, for whom, and how it is used.

Good design is not only about what a tool can do. It is also about what it should do, when, and under whose control.

Foundations to make it safe:

- Consent- clear, ongoing, and reversible: User controls what is collected, when, and with whom it is shared. Sharing is reversible.
- Human handover by design: Clear, fast paths to real people in tough moments. The system knows its limits.
- Privacy and data stewardship: Where possible, sensitive processing stays on the device, least data needed to help is collected, strong data encryptions and retention policies.

- Plain-language transparency: User can see why a suggestion appeared and easily turn any feature off.
- Fairness, inclusion, and culture: Mental health language varies across cultures, ages, and identities. Tools must work for local languages/voices, not only for those most represented in the data.
- No nudges for profit: Well-being goals, not engagement goals. If revenue depends on attention, ethics will suffer. Choose models aligned with health, not clicks.
- Accountability and governance: Define roles. Developers, providers, clinicians, and purchasers should each hold clear duties. Publish readable "model cards" and "data cards" outlining training data sources, intended use, and known limits. Align with legal and health privacy rules

Finally, clear regulatory frameworks are essential to ensure accountability and ethical use for cautious integration of AI tools in mental health care.

By thoughtfully addressing the challenges while shaping tomorrow's solutions, we can harness the potential of AI to improve the accessibility, effectiveness, and ethical use of mental healthcare.

But even then, one question lingers:

Are we at a risk of losing our intuitive ability?

Not in the realm of professional help where access, scale, and consistency are urgent needs, but in the everyday. Will constant reliance on tools distance us from our own ability to sense, connect, and understand?

We have apps reminding us to drink water, to stand, or tell us our heart is beating is fast. Are we getting more disconnected from ourselves? Do we truly need more tools, or do we sometimes need space away from them? Could reliance on constant prompts gradually weaken the very intuitive insights that help us notice a friend's silence, sense our own tension, or repair a fragile relationship?

If AI begins to assess our social interactions, how will that change the way we connect, communicate, and trust? Will it erode the quiet human skills of listening, noticing, and being present?

The promise is tempting: fewer misunderstandings, deeper empathy, more supportive relationships. But the risks are equally clear: blurred boundaries, loss of privacy, and the pressure of being emotionally "read" at all times.

The future may not be about whether this becomes possible, but how we choose to use it and whether we can hold on to our own self-awareness while allowing machines to support it.

Can the next wave be built with people at the centre, and AI respectfully at the edges?

If you were developing such a tool,

- What red lines would you set for AI in emotional care?
- When should a digital companion stop, and a human take over?
- What evidence would you need to recommend such a tool to a friend, a student, or a patient?
- How will your organization align incentives so that well-being, not engagement drives design?

A Closing Picture

Imagine a world where asking for help feels as normal as charging your phone.

Where a kind prompt helps you pause.

Where rest is built as part of doing good work.

Where cities offer quiet corners the way they offer benches and lights.

Where, when life gets heavy, the path to a human is short and clear.

Questions to carry forward:

- What if every day mental care felt as normal as a stretch break?
- Could a small nudge at the right time turn hard days softer, for you and those around you?
- What if technology helped us practise empathy, not replace it?

- What would it mean if our devices encouraged reflection before reaction?
- What if the next wave of AI made communities warmer, not just smarter?

Perhaps the real question is:

Can we design AI in a way that helps us become better-for ourselves, and for one another?

References

1. American Psychiatric Association. (2024, May 22). New polling data shows most employers offer some form of mental health benefits, but burnout impacts over 40% of employees. https://www.psychiatry.org/news-room/news-releases/new-polling-data-on-workplace-mental-health
2. Bassett, C. The computational therapeutic: exploring Weizenbaum's ELIZA as a history of the present. AI & Soc 34, 803–812 (2019). https://doi.org/10.1007/s00146-018-0825-9
3. Fitzpatrick K, Darcy A, Vierhile M. Delivering Cognitive Behavior Therapy to Young Adults With Symptoms of Depression and Anxiety Using a Fully Automated Conversational Agent (Woebot): A Randomized Controlled Trial. JMIR Ment Health 2017;4(2):e19. https://mental.jmir.org/2017/2/e19
4. Grand View Research. (2024). AI In Mental Health Market Size, Share & Trends Analysis Report By Offering (Software, Services), By Technology (ML, NLP), By Disorder, By Region, And Segment Forecasts, 2024 – 2030. https://www.grandviewresearch.com/industry-analysis/ai-mental-health-market-report
5. IndiaTimes. (2025). American woman, 29, dies by suicide after talking to AI instead of a therapist; mother uncovers truth 6 months later. IndiaTimes.

https://indiatimes.com/trending/american-woman-29-dies-by-suicide-after-talking-to-ai-instead-of-a-therapist-mother-uncovers-truth-6-months-after-her-death-667398.html

6. Kang, M., & Chai, K. (2022). Wearable sensing systems for monitoring mental health. Sensors, 22(3), 994. https://doi.org/10.3390/s22030994

7. Khare, S. K., Blanes-Vidal, V., Nadimi, E. S., & Acharya, U. R. (2024). Emotion recognition and artificial intelligence: a systematic review (2014–2023) and research recommendations. Information Fusion, 102, 102019. https://doi.org/10.1016/j.inffus.2023.102019

8. Olawade, D. B., Wada, O. Z., Odetayo, A., DavidOlawade, A. C., Asaolu, F., & Eberhardt, J. (2024). Enhancing Mental Health with Artificial Intelligence: Current Trends and Future Prospects. Journal of Medicine, Surgery, and Public Health, 3, 100099. https://doi.org/10.1016/j.glmedi.2024.100099

9. Rowshani, C. (2023, June 9). Why Global Mental Health Benefits Matter for a Distributed Workforce. Spring Health Blog. https://springhealth.com/blog/global-mental-health-benefits-for-distributed-workforce

10. Sentio. (2025, March). ChatGPT may be the largest provider of mental health support in the United States. Sentio Survey Report. https://sentio.org/ai-research/ai-survey

11. The Latest Mental Health Statistics: What the Numbers Say About the State of Our Minds in 2024. (2024, August 13). Huntington Psychology. https://huntingtonpsych.com/blog/the-latest-mental-health-statistics-what-the-numbers-say-about-the-state-of-our-minds-in-2024

12. World Health Organization. Social isolation and loneliness. https://www.who.int/teams/social-determinants-of-health/demographic-change-and-healthy-ageing/social-isolation-and-loneliness

13. Zhou, S., Zhao, J., & Zhang, L. Application of Artificial Intelligence on Psychological Interventions and Diagnosis: An Overview. Front. Psychiatry, 13(2022), https://doi.org/10.3389/fpsyt.2022.811665

Probabilistic AI: Navigating Uncertainty

By Jitendra Bikram Shah*

> *"Do not bet everything on one future. Think in ranges, update with evidence, and navigate."*

The Comfort of Certainty

Imagine yourself standing at the edge of a wide, open field. A soft fog covers everything ahead, creating a sense of mystery and anticipation. Somewhere out there, there is a cozy cabin where you can rest. The air feels cold. Your breath turns to mist. You can hear wind in the tall grass, but you cannot see far.

You have a compass; its needle is fixed on north. You could glance at it once, fix that direction in your mind, and march forward with the unwavering conviction that

---

*Jitendra Bikram Shah is an experienced technology architect with over 20 years of expertise in software and quality engineering. He has demonstrated a strong ability to drive innovation and support business growth by leading teams in software and automation initiatives. Passionate about advancing emerging technologies, especially in AI/ML, he focuses on the transformative potential of Generative AI.

DOI: 10.1201/9781003737803-3

you "know where you are going." Or you could admit a more uncomfortable reality: the path might twist unexpectedly, hidden streams and ditches may block your way, and even your compass might lie if magnetic deposits beneath the soil bend their readings.

Most people, given no time to reflect, choose the first option. We cling to certainty because it feels safe.

For a long time, psychologists have observed that certainty offers emotional comfort when faced with complexity. It is the mental equivalent of a thick blanket on a cold night, a stabilizing sensation even if the blanket is a little worn at the edges[17]. This craving for closure and clear answers is so embedded in human cognition that it shapes decisions in business, politics, and personal life alike[29].

If you are planning a beach vacation, you want "It will be sunny," not "There is a 65% chance of sun, 25% chance of clouds, and 10% chance of rain." If you are running a company, you want "Sales will grow 8%," not "There is a 70% probability growth will fall between 4% and 12%." As Daniel Kahneman, Nobel laureate in economics, observed, our minds are "machines for jumping to conclusions"[17]. Given partial information, we eagerly fill in the gaps with a clean story, even when reality is uncertain and messy.

This tendency creates what cognitive scientists call the illusion of certainty[9,28], the false sense that a neatly packaged prediction is somehow more accurate than a range of possibilities. In organizations, the leader who declares "We will achieve X" is often rewarded for their confidence, even if the more truthful answer is "There is a 70% chance we will achieve X if certain conditions hold."

Artificial intelligence, in its early modern wave, supercharged this illusion. Early deep learning systems labeled images with "99.9% confidence," translated languages with remarkable accuracy, and recommended products so precisely that it felt as though they could not fail. Yet that 99.9% "confidence" was an internal statistical output, not a guarantee of truth. And when these systems faced inputs outside their training data, so-called "out-of-distribution" scenarios, they could collapse into absurd or dangerous errors[1].

The danger is not in uncertainty itself, but in pretending it does not exist. History shows that when we build systems, human or machine, on the assumption of flawless predictability, the cracks only appear when it is too late to react.

When Certainty Broke

Human history is littered with the wreckage of overconfidence. Repeatedly, the same pattern emerges:

1. Someone builds a model, rule, or belief that works brilliantly at first.
2. Success hardens into blind trust.
3. The world changes in ways the model never accounted for.
4. With no flexibility built in, the system collapses.

One of the clearest examples unfolded in 1998, inside the high-gloss offices of Long-Term Capital Management (LTCM). Staffed by two Nobel Prize–winning economists and some of the most celebrated traders in finance, LTCM was considered a "dream team" of market prediction[22]. Their secret weapon was a set of sophisticated mathematical models that exploited tiny, temporary mispricing between related securities. The assumption was critical but straightforward: correlations between asset prices would remain within the limits observed in decades of historical data.

At first, the model printed money. Confidence grew. Leverage ballooned. Then the Russian government defaulted on its debt, and global investors stampeded into "safe" U.S. Treasury bonds. Asset correlations swung wildly outside their historical range. The model's core assumption, that such a swing was virtually impossible, was shredded. Losses mounted so fast that the Federal Reserve orchestrated a $3.6 billion private-sector bailout to prevent wider market collapse[8].

A decade later, the same overconfidence reemerged in a different costume. This time it was a formula, the Gaussian copula, used to price mortgage-backed securities. The formula boiled down the messy relationships between thousands of home loans into a single, reassuring correlation number[21]. Rating agencies stamped AAA on billions in securities. The hidden flaw: it assumed that housing markets in different regions were largely independent. When national lending practices and low interest rates bound them tightly together, the correlation spiked, defaults cascaded, and the Great Financial Crisis of 2008 followed[7].

This bias toward single, tidy numbers is not confined to finance. In early 2020, as COVID-19 spread globally, governments desperately wanted to know: How many will be infected? How many will die? When will the peak hit? Models were rushed out with bold point estimates based on incomplete, inconsistent data[14]. When reality inevitably diverged, public trust in both the models and the institutions using them eroded, a crisis of confidence layered on top of a public health emergency.

The stakes are just as high in engineered systems. In 1977, two Boeing 747s collided on the fog-shrouded runway at Tenerife Airport after each crew acted with certainty on incomplete information. It remains the deadliest accident in aviation history[15]. In 1986, the Space Shuttle Challenger disintegrated shortly after liftoff, partly because NASA managers treated "it has not failed before" as proof that it could not fail now, ignoring engineering warnings about O-ring seals in cold weather[31].

Different domains. Same trap. Overconfidence in a single model, forecast, or belief, and an unwillingness to grapple with uncertainty, turn small cracks into catastrophic failures.

The lesson from these failures is not that models are useless, but that certainty is brittle. The more complex and interconnected the world becomes, the faster brittle systems crack. The alternative is not to throw away our compasses, but to upgrade them, to move from pointing in one direction and hoping, to mapping a range of possible terrains and preparing for each.

We humans have a deep craving for single, clean answers. If your boss asks when a project will be finished, "October 14th" feels safe and solid; "between October 12th and 21st, unless supply chain delays push it into November" feels slippery. Yet the second answer is more truthful, and in the long run, more useful. It forces you to prepare for scenarios rather than cling to a promise.

So, what replaces brittle certainty?

Why Probabilities Beat Single Numbers

This is the essence of probabilistic thinking: replacing point estimates with probability distributions. Instead of "sales will grow 8%," we say, "There is a 10% chance growth will be under 5%, a 60% chance it will be between 5% and 10%, and a 30% chance it will be over 10%." The distribution not only shows the most likely outcome, but also the spread, where risk hides, where upside lives, and how uncertain the forecast really is.

How do we update those probabilities as evidence arrives?

Bayes' Rule: Updating Your Beliefs.

The Simple Math Behind "Learning from Evidence"

Out on the foggy plain, you do not pick a direction once. You notice signs, the sound of water, a shift in the wind, and you update your path. Probabilistic thinking is the habit of updating. The simple math under the hood has a name: Bayes' Rule[3,4,25].

Bayes' Rule says: start with a belief, see new evidence, then update your belief. Your starting belief is the prior. Your new belief is the posterior. How much you move depends on how strong and reliable is the evidence[3,4,25].

In symbols:

$$P(A|B) = \frac{P(B|A) \times P(A)}{P(B)}$$

In plain words: P(A) Prior: what you believed before you looked again. P(B) Evidence: what you just saw or measured. P(B|A) Likelihood: how often that evidence shows up when your belief is true. And P(A|B) Posterior: your new belief after considering the evidence[3,4,25].

A quick everyday example. There is a 20% chance it will rain today (20 out of 100 days like this). Dark clouds roll in. Suppose dark clouds appear on 80 out of 100 rainy days, but also on 30 out of 100 dry days. Out of 100 days like this:

- 20 are rainy; clouds on 16 of those.
- 80 are dry; clouds on 24 of those.
- Total cloudy days: 40.

So the chance of rain given clouds is 16 out of 40, which is 40%. Your belief doubles from 20% to 40%. You still do not "know," but you pack a raincoat.

A quick business example. Your team says 10 out of 100 leads usually buy (10%). You notice that leads who opened last week's email are more serious. In past data, 60 out of 100 buyers opened that email, but 20 out of 100 non-buyers opened it too. Out of 100 leads:

- 10 buys; 6 of those opened.
- 90 do not buy; 18 of those opened.
- Total who opened: 24.

So the chance of a sale given an open is 6 out of 24, which is 25%. You invest more time in those leads.

Key idea: strong, trustworthy evidence moves your belief a lot. Weak or noisy evidence moves it a little. Also, watch base rates (how familiar something is to begin with). When something is rare, even a good test can raise many false alarms[1,17,29].

This is what your "instrument" does in the fog. It does not hand you certainty. It helps you update, step by step, as new signs appear[3,4].

That distribution mindset builds resilience. If a weather app tells you "72°F and sunny," you will pack only sunglasses. If it tells you "60% chance of sun in the 70s, 30% chance of rain in the 50s, 10% chance of thunderstorms," you will also pack a rain jacket. You arrive prepared for multiple futures.

Artificial intelligence magnifies both the problem of false certainty and the opportunity for calibrated confidence. Classic AI models, especially early deep learning systems, often output a single label with a confidence score: cat (99.9%), tumor present (95%), approve loan (98%). The number looks precise, but it is an internal measure, not an ironclad truth[12]. When these models encounter inputs outside their training data, their confidence scores can be disastrously misleading.

Probabilistic AI systems handle uncertainty by generating distributions over potential outcomes instead of a single best guess. In medical diagnostics, a Bayesian neural network might state, "There is an 80% chance this is pneumonia, but uncertainty is high due to poor image quality," prompting a second human review. In self-driving cars, probabilistic perception models forecast not only where another vehicle is heading but also the range of possible paths it might follow, along with the likelihood of each, before deciding whether to brake or accelerate[18].

The difference is subtle but profound. A deterministic AI says, "This is the future." A probabilistic AI says, "Here are several possible futures, here is how likely each is, and here is how confident I am in that assessment." One locks you into a single staircase. The other hand gives you a suspension bridge that can sway, adapt, and keep you upright when the ground shifts.

Two Kinds of Uncertainty: Aleatoric and Epistemic

Learning to live with uncertainty begins with understanding what kind of uncertainty you are facing. Not all fog is the same. Some is baked into the world itself, randomness you can never remove. Other fog exists only because you have not looked closely enough yet. AI researchers call these two kinds *aleatoric* and *epistemic* uncertainty[6].

Aleatoric uncertainty is built-in randomness, the "dice roll." No matter how many times you roll, you cannot know the exact next outcome. The weather will always have an element of this; even with perfect instruments, you cannot pinpoint the precise moment a raindrop will hit your head. AI models see it in the spread of responses when two people with the same medical condition react differently to the same treatment. You cannot eliminate it; you design to withstand it.

Epistemic uncertainty is the uncertainty of ignorance ("we do not know yet"). It comes from missing knowledge, the fog that clears when you gather more data. If a self-driving car has never seen snow, its uncertainty about how to handle icy roads is epistemic. Train it in snowy conditions, and that uncertainty shrinks. In finance, forecasting an emerging market without historical data carries huge epistemic uncertainty, and can be reduced by collecting more relevant data.

Treating one type as the other can be costly. Trying to "eliminate" aleatoric uncertainty wastes resources on the impossible. Ignoring epistemic uncertainty leaves you vulnerable when you could have learned more. Skilled decision-makers and skilled AI systems manage both at once.

Uncertainty is not only about what is true today. It is also about what could happen if we act.

From Patterns to What-Ifs: The Ladder of Causation

To move from spotting patterns to testing actions to imagining alternate pasts, we need tools that can reason about cause and effect and ask, "What if?" Researchers like Judea Pearl call this climb the "ladder of causation", from patterns, to interventions, to what-ifs[26]. Here is how that ladder works.

On the lowest rung is *association*: seeing patterns. "When the sky darkens, it often rains." This is where most machine learning lives, spotting statistical links without knowing why.

The next rung is *intervention*: doing something to see what happens. "If I carry an umbrella, will I stay dry?" It is cause-and-effect, the domain of controlled experiments and A/B tests.

The highest rung is *counterfactuals*: imagining alternate pasts. "If the patient had received treatment earlier, would they have survived?" Counterfactual reasoning allows both humans and advanced AI to ask "what if" questions, a crucial step in planning and ethics.

Most AI systems today are stuck on the first rung. They are brilliant pattern-matchers but poor at predicting how the world will change when we change something. The next wave of probabilistic AI aims to climb higher, simulating interventions and weighing alternate histories before acting.

This shift matters because the world is not static. Cause-and-effect chains change when we push on them. If we can teach machines to model not just the patterns of the past but the possible branches of the future, we can prepare for surprises rather than be blindsided by them.

And that is where probabilistic architectures, Bayesian neural networks, generative models, and probabilistic programming stop being academic toys and start being survival tools.

To use this ladder well, we need machines that know what they do not know.

How Machines Use Uncertainty

Once you start thinking in terms of uncertainty, the question becomes: how do you build machines that can think this way, too? For years, early AI behaved like overconfident students, consistently producing a single, crisp answer, even when they were guessing. That decisiveness made them easy to use but dangerous to trust.

Probabilistic AI changes that. At its heart are models that do not just give an answer, but also tell you how sure they are, and what might make them wrong. One way they do this is through **Bayesian neural networks** (BNNs)[23]. Instead of treating each learned weight inside the network as a fixed number, BNNs treat them as probability distributions: "it is probably here, but it could be higher or lower." Each time the model makes a prediction, it samples from those distributions, runs the input, and records the spread of outcomes. That spread is as important as the prediction itself.

When a medical image classifier sees a blurry X-ray, a deterministic model might still say "pneumonia" with absolute confidence. A BNN can say, "80% chance of pneumonia, but uncertainty is high due to poor image quality." That uncertainty flag can be the difference between a doctor acting immediately or ordering more tests.

Another branch of probabilistic AI focuses on imagining, not just predicting. These *generative models* learn the shape of the data they have seen so well that they can create new, realistic possibilities from scratch. Variational autoencoders compress data into a probabilistic "latent space" and then reconstruct it, allowing them to generate new but plausible examples[20]. GANs, which pit two networks against each other in a game of forgery and detection, can produce satellite imagery of regions that have not been mapped[11]. Diffusion models, which begin with pure noise and gradually sculpt it into a coherent image, power many of today's creative AI tools[13]; however, they can also be employed to mimic weather patterns or disease spread under different assumptions.

The real power comes when these imagination engines are paired with *transformer-based language models* like GPT, which already operate probabilistically at their core[30]. Every time they generate text, they assign a probability to each possible next word. You can take the most likely sequence, produce a safe, predictable answer, or explore other high-probability branches to surface alternative scenarios. This makes them natural companions for scenario planning, allowing them to spin out multiple coherent futures from the same starting point.

The final piece is accessibility. Until recently, building a probabilistic model required heavy statistical expertise. Now, *probabilistic programming languages* such as Stan, Pyro, and TensorFlow Probability allow data scientists to describe problems in code the way they'd sketch them on a whiteboard[5]. The software handles the hard math of inference, lowering the barrier for building systems that embrace uncertainty.

Together, these advances are changing how AI works in the real world. A finance system can model not just expected returns, but the full distribution of risks. A healthcare model can update survival curves in real time as new patient data arrives. A self-driving car can weigh multiple possible trajectories for every vehicle it sees and hesitates when its uncertainty spikes.

It is not about AI as a crystal ball. It is about AI as a mapmaker, mapping out not just one path ahead, but a network of possible routes, each with its own probabilities and warning signs.

These tools are essential because real decisions involve real stakes.

Where It Matters: Finance, Health, Autonomy, Policy

The accurate measure of any philosophy is not in conference slides but in the messy, unpredictable reality of real-world decisions. Probabilistic AI has moved beyond research papers into domains where uncertainty is not an inconvenience; it is the air people breathe.

In *finance*, old-school risk models assumed markets followed tidy bell curves. This made life easy for analysts but ignored the fat tails, the extreme events that happen far more often than the math predicted[24]. When those rare-but-not-rare-enough events hit, portfolios built on false certainty collapsed. Probabilistic models change the conversation. A deterministic forecast might say, "Investment A will yield 5%, Investment B will yield 6%; choose B." A probabilistic model instead says, "Investment A has a 70% chance of moderate gain, 30% chance of small loss. Investment B has equal odds of high gain or deep loss." Suddenly, the decision is not about chasing a number; it is about aligning with your risk appetite.

In *healthcare*, treatment decisions have long been guided by population averages. That works when you are prescribing aspirin, but not when you are deciding whether to pursue aggressive cancer treatment. A probabilistic model can integrate a patient's genomic data, scan results, and history to produce survival curves for each treatment path[27]. The doctor can sit down and say, "Treatment A gives a 60% chance of surviving three years, Treatment B offers 75% but carries higher side-effect risks, Treatment C is gentler but less effective." Instead of a yes/no answer, the patient gets a map of possible futures and the dignity of informed choice.

For *autonomous systems* like self-driving cars, the cost of false certainty is physical harm. Early rule-based systems worked fine in controlled environments, but failed spectacularly in novel situations, such as a construction site or a cyclist weaving between cars. Modern probabilistic perception models assign probabilities to every possible trajectory of nearby vehicles and pedestrians[19]. They also monitor their own uncertainty; if epistemic uncertainty spikes because the scene is unlike anything in training, the car can slow, stop, or request human intervention.

Even in **public policy and climate science**, where non-experts often consume predictions, probabilistic approaches matter. A single forecast like "GDP will grow 2.3%" hides enormous uncertainty. Probabilistic models can present distributions "50% chance GDP grows 1–3%, 30% chance slower growth, 20% chance contraction" paired with scenario narratives about what could drive each outcome[16]. It is less comforting, but it is more truthful and more helpful in crafting adaptive policy.

In each of these domains, the shift is the same: from a single staircase to a suspension bridge that sways with the wind but keeps standing.

Models help, but people make choices.

People and Culture: Learning to Live with Uncertainty

We like to imagine that more innovative models alone will fix our decisions. But the bottleneck is not only in the code; it is also in us.

Human beings did not evolve to love probability. On the savanna, the cost of hesitation could be death. If the grass rustled, you did not calculate odds; you ran. That survival wiring still hums under our modern habits. We prefer the single story. We crave the clean forecast. We reward the leader who sounds certain, even when the world will not cooperate[31].

Ambiguity makes many of us uncomfortable. Faced with a known 50% chance or an unknown 40–60% range, most people choose the known bet even if the unknown could be better. Psychologists call this *ambiguity aversion*[29]. It is why a single number calms us more than a distribution. It is why "We will deliver by October 14" wins more applause than "There is a 70% chance we will finish by mid-October, unless our supplier slips." The applause is genuine. The confidence is not.

There is also the *narrative fallacy*, our talent for shrinking a complex, multi-cause event into a straightforward explanation. "Stocks rose because of this headline." "Sales fell because the ad campaign failed." Sometimes it is partly true. Often it is tidy fiction. Our brains choose story over statistics because stories fit in a breath; statistics ask for a breath and a pause[10].

And then there is *overconfidence*. Ask a room full of smart people for a 90% confidence interval on a number, say, the population of Japan, and many will miss wildly. Their ranges are too narrow. Their gut feels more certain than the data supports[1]. That same narrow gut builds narrow plans, and narrow plans break.

Organizations often make these biases worse, not better. Boardrooms want exact delivery dates because other teams depend on them. Politicians announce single-number targets because “there is a 70% chance” sounds weak on a podium. Quarterly incentives reward leaders who project certainty even when uncertainty is the only honest stance. Somewhere between a model that outputs a lovely probability distribution and a decision memo that lands on an executive’s desk, the distribution gets boiled down to one number, precision without truth.

Changing that pattern does not require turning everyone into statisticians. It requires building *probability literacy*, a shared language for uncertainty that leaders, managers, and teams can use together. Three habits carry most of the weight:

Read distributions, not just points. Know the difference between mean and median. Notice skew. Understand that a 95% interval is not a promise: it is a guide. When you see a fan chart instead of a line, do not ask, “Which is it?” Ask “What is likely, what is risky, and what would change the picture?”

Interrogate assumptions. Every model sits on scaffolding: data sources, priors, causal stories. Ask “What is driving this estimate?” “Where are we blind?” “What scenarios could break this forecast?” You are not tearing the model down. You are stress-testing the bridge before you drive a convoy over it.

Reward process, not just outcomes. In a probabilistic world, good decisions can have bad consequences, and bad decisions can get lucky. Judges' decisions are based on whether they were well-calibrated to the information available at the time. That is how you build cultures that tell the truth about uncertainty without punishing honesty[28].

Ironically, *probabilistic AI can teach this literacy back to us*. When systems surface not just a prediction but its confidence, and when teams see, week after week, how those uncertainties resolve, people develop intuition for ranges. They start saying things like, "We're in the fat tail," or "Confidence is low because we're out of distribution." It becomes normal to plan for several futures instead of one. Tools change minds when they change meetings.

Because those choices affect people, ethics and rules matter.

Ethics and Accountability

But probability has an *ethical edge*. It forces us to confront hard questions we cannot finesse with a neat single number.

Justice. If a risk tool estimates that Person A has an 80% chance of reoffending and Person B has 75%, should those five percentage points change sentencing or parole? What if the data feeding the model comes from historically biased policing patterns? Courts and communities need transparency standards: what data went in, what fairness constraints were enforced, how uncertainty is communicated, and how humans can override the machine when judgment and mercy demand it[2].

Medicine. How does a doctor tell a patient, "You have a 30% chance of surviving five years"? Accuracy matters, but so does how people hear numbers. Some will seize the 30% as hope. Others will feel crushed. Good practice blends calibrated facts with compassionate framing: "Here are the odds, here is what could improve them, and here is how we will decide together." Communication guides matter just as much as models[27].

Autonomy and responsibility. If a self-driving system calculates a maneuver has a 0.05% chance of collision, takes it, and the rare event happens, who is responsible: the manufacturer, the fleet operator, the software team, or the owner? The answer lives in policy, not math alone. We need legal frameworks that match probabilistic decision-making where risk thresholds are explicit, audits are possible, and accountability does not vanish into "the model decided"[18].

Across sectors, *governance* must evolve documentation of model purpose and training data; independent red-team testing for distribution shifts; hotlines in code for "I do not know" states; human-in-the-loop controls with clear escalation paths; and dashboards that show leaders not just the answer, but the *confidence and the caveats*. Institutions will need new roles, part statistician, part ethicist, part product thinker, whose job is to assure that uncertainty is surfaced, not smoothed away.

What does this look like on the ground?

Three Rooms: Uncertainty in Practice

Now bring the lens closer. Imagine three rooms on the same morning.

In the first, a hospital conference room, a physician and a patient sit shoulder to shoulder, not across a desk. On the screen: three treatment paths, three survival curves, three bands of uncertainty. The doctor says, "These are the odds. Here is what could shift them. Here is what matters to you. Let us decide together." The patient is not being told what will happen. They are being invited to choose across futures, with eyes open[27].

In the second, a control center for a fleet of autonomous shuttles. A storm rolls in. The system's epistemic uncertainty spikes, and the cameras are seeing conditions they were not trained on. The dashboard flashes: "Confidence degraded on Routes 4 and 7. Slowing to 20 mph or rerouting recommended." A human supervisor approves the slowdown. Some trips take longer. None ends badly[18].

In the third, a policy war-room. A minister looks at a carbon pricing proposal. The old way would show one GDP forecast, one emissions forecast, and one neat headline. The new dashboard shows a *fan*: median emissions drop of 10% by 2035, a 25% chance of under 5%, a 15% chance of over 15%, with notes on assumptions, technology costs, consumer behavior, and international coordination. The minister asks, "What policy portfolio performs across these futures?" The answer is an *adaptive plan*; triggers that deepen measures if the median misses, safety nets if the economy stumbles, and rapid scaling if innovation arrives faster than expected[16].

In all three rooms, the melody is the same: transparency about uncertainty, choices designed for multiple futures, and humans who refuse to pretend fog is clear sky. That melody only plays if we reset what "good leadership" sounds like.

Conclusion: Crossing the Fog

Now, back to the traveler in the fog.

Which brings us back to you, standing on the edge of that foggy plain from the beginning of this chapter.

The fog has not lifted. The wind still moves the grass. The cabin is still out there somewhere. But something has changed. You are not holding a compass that lies with a single arrow. You are holding a different instrument, one that shows a *fan of bearings*. Some paths have a thick band of probability. Others are thinner. Some routes flicker with a warning: low confidence, unknown terrain. The instrument does not command; it informs. It does not flatter with certainty; it equips with clarity.

You take a few steps. The ground is uneven, but your weight adjusts. You veer slightly to the east, where the band is stronger. A few minutes later, a dark shape looms: a boulder, invisible until you are close. You check your instrument. The bands update as you circle. The path curves around, then straightens. A hundred minor course corrections, each one too small to boast about, together keep you from walking off a ridge.

Behind you stretches the route you could have walked: a straight gouge across the grass where someone who "knew the way" marched into a ditch and then tried to climb out. Their line looks decisive. It is also wrong.

The suspension bridge metaphor lives in your legs now. *Deterministic thinking* was a staircase, narrow, precise, brittle. It invited you to trust where you placed your feet, until the ground shifted, and then it left you in the air. *Probabilistic thinking* is a bridge that moves as you move, unnerving at first, but faithful when the winds arrive. The movement is not a weakness; it is how the bridge survives.

You could pause and listen. Out in the fog, you hear other travelers. Some are shouting their certainties into the mist: "This way!" "That way!" Some have built little staircases and are carrying them, step by step, until the steps no longer fit. But others, a growing number, are moving more quietly, checking their instruments, calling out their confidence and their doubts: "Strong bearing to the northwest." "Low confidence on the ridge." "Collecting more data before crossing the stream." You are not alone.

And now you notice something else. You are not just a traveler. You are also a builder. Every choice you make, the tools you adopt, the dashboards you demand, the way you run your meetings, the way you communicate risk to your teams and stakeholders, lays planks in a bridge others will walk. If you reward false certainty, you will get more of it. If you reward calibrated confidence, you will get plans that bend and hold.

This is what probabilistic AI offers when we use it well. Not a crystal ball, but a *compass with humility*. Not the illusion of control, but the practice of *continuous course correction*. Not a promise to erase uncertainty, but the discipline to face it, quantify it, and design with it.

The century ahead will not be stingy with fog. Climate shocks will redraw maps. Supply chains will tangle. Politics will lurch. Technologies will leap, surprise, and sometimes fail. In that world, what you need is not bravado, but *resilience with a brain*, strategies that work across a range of futures and instruments that tell you when to slow down, when to learn more, and when to steer hard.

You look up. The mist thins for a moment. Far ahead, you glimpse a warm, amber light. It might be the cabin. It might be reflected in the sky. You do not bet everything on that glimmer. You take another measurement. You listen. You ask a question you have learned to love: "What could happen next, and how ready am I for each path?" Then you keep moving, not because you know, but because you are ready *not to know*.

We will not always get it right. Some days, the fog will thicken. Some choices will hurt. But with probabilistic tools in hand and a culture that treats uncertainty as information, we will not be brittle. We will be bendable. We will keep our footing when the ground shifts.

And that is enough to cross a continent of fog.

We can pack differently. We can plan differently. We can lead differently. We can build machines that tell us not just what they think but how sure they are, and we can create institutions that listen to those caveats instead of sending them away.

We can stop pretending that uncertainty is not there. We can stop rewarding the loudest staircase. We can start rewarding the steadiest bridge.

We can teach young teams to love distributions. We can teach executives to ask for ranges. We can teach our dashboards to blush when they are out of their depth. We can write policies that name acceptable risk, audit our models for bias and drift, and anchor accountability where it belongs with us.

The fog will not end. But the fear can.

Because once you have learned to navigate, fog is not the enemy. It is the setting.

We cannot predict it all. We cannot control it all. But we can navigate what comes with calibrated confidence; human judgment amplified by machines that know their limits, organizations that tell the truth about uncertainty, and a culture that understands the wisdom of saying, "I do not know, yet."

And when we do, the cabin is not just a place we hope to stumble into. It is a path we can reach by steering, adjusting, and choosing well repeatedly.

"Trade certainty for calibrated confidence. We cannot predict the future, but we can navigate it."

References

1. Amodei, D., Olah, C., Steinhardt, J., Christiano, P., Schulman, J., & Mané, D. (2016). Concrete Problems in AI Safety (arXiv:1606.06565). arXiv. https://doi.org/10.48550/arXiv.1606.06565
2. Barocas, S., Hardt, M., & Narayanan, A. (2023). Fairness and Machine Learning. fairmlbook.org (open textbook).
3. Bayes, T. (1763). An Essay towards solving a Problem in the Doctrine of Chances. Philosophical Transactions of the Royal Society of London, 53, 370–418. (Posthumously edited by Richard Price.)
4. Bishop, C. M. (2006). Pattern Recognition and Machine Learning. Springer.
5. Carpenter, B., Gelman, A., Hoffman, M. D., Lee, D., Goodrich, B., Betancourt, M., Brubaker, M. A., Guo, J., Li, P., & Riddell, A. (2017). Stan: A Probabilistic Programming Language. Journal of Statistical Software, 76, 1. https://doi.org/10.18637/jss.v076.i01
6. Der Kiureghian, A., & Ditlevsen, O. (2009). Aleatory or epistemic? Does it matter? Structural Safety, 31(2), 105–112.
7. Financial Crisis Inquiry Commission. (2011). The Financial Crisis Inquiry Report. U.S. Government Printing Office.
8. Fleming, M., & Liu, W. (n.d.). Near Failure of Long-Term Capital Management. Retrieved August 16, 2025, from https://www.federalreservehistory.org/essays/ltcm-near-failure
9. Gigerenzer, G. (2015). Calculated risks: How to know when numbers deceive you. Simon and Schuster.

10. Gigerenzer, G. (2007). Gut Feelings: The Intelligence of the Unconscious. Viking.

11. Goodfellow, I. J., Pouget-Abadie, J., Mirza, M., Xu, B., Warde-Farley, D., Ozair, S., Courville, A., & Bengio, Y. (2014). Generative adversarial nets. Proceedings of the 28th International Conference on Neural Information Processing Systems - Volume 2, 2, 2672–2680.

12. Guo, C., Pleiss, G., Sun, Y., & Weinberger, K. Q. (2017). On Calibration of Modern Neural Networks. Proceedings of ICML, PMLR 70:1321–1330.

13. Ho, J., Jain, A., & Abbeel, P. (2020). Denoising Diffusion Probabilistic Models. NeurIPS, 33.

14. Holmdahl, I., & Buckee, C. (2020). Wrong but Useful , What COVID-19 Epidemiologic Models Can and Cannot Tell Us. New England Journal of Medicine, 383(4), 303–305.

15. ICAO. (1978). Aircraft Accident Digest No. 19. International Civil Aviation Organization.

16. IPCC (2023). AR6 Synthesis Report: Climate Change 2023. Intergovernmental Panel on Climate Change.

17. Kahneman, D. (2011). Thinking, Fast and Slow. Farrar, Straus and Giroux.

18. Kendall, A., & Gal, Y. (2017). What Uncertainties Do We Need in Bayesian Deep Learning for Computer Vision? Advances in Neural Information Processing Systems, 30.

19. Kendall, A., Gal, Y., & Cipolla, R. (2018). Multi-task Learning Using Uncertainty to Weigh Losses for Scene Geometry and Semantics. CVPR.

20. Kingma, D. P., & Welling, M. (2013). Auto-Encoding Variational Bayes. arXiv:1312.6114.

21. Li, D. X. (2000). On Default Correlation: A Copula Function Approach. The Journal of Fixed Income, 9(4), 43–54.

22. Lowenstein, R. (2000). When Genius Failed: The Rise and Fall of Long-Term Capital Management. Random House.

23. MacKay, D. J. C. (1992). A practical Bayesian framework for backpropagation networks. Neural Computation, 4(3), 448–472.

24. Mandelbrot, B., & Hudson, R. L. (2004). The (Mis)Behavior of Markets: A Fractal View of Financial Turbulence. Basic Books.

25. Mismar, H., Shamayleh, A., & Qazi, A. (2022). Prioritizing Risks in Last Mile Delivery: A Bayesian Belief Network Approach. IEEE Access, 10, 118551–118562.

26. Pearl, J., & Mackenzie, D. (2018). The Book of Why: The New Science of Cause and Effect. Basic Books.

27. Schwalbe, N., & Wahl, B. (2020). Artificial intelligence and the future of global health. The Lancet, 395(10236), 1579–1586.

28. Tetlock, P., & Gardner, D. (2015). Superforecasting: The Art and Science of Prediction. Crown.

29. Tversky, A., & Kahneman, D. (1974). Judgment under Uncertainty: Heuristics and Biases. Science, 185(4157), 1124–1131.

30. Vaswani, A., Shazeer, N., Parmar, N., Uszkoreit, J., Jones, L., Gomez, A. N., Kaiser, L., & Polosukhin, I. (2023). Attention Is All You Need (arXiv:1706.03762). arXiv. https://doi.org/10.48550/arXiv.1706.03762

31. Vaughan, D. (1996). The Challenger Launch Decision: Risky Technology, Culture, and Deviance at NASA. University of Chicago Press.

The Intelligent Journey

By Joshua Lau Boon Wei[*]

An Intelligent Journey Awaits

Even before your suitcase is packed, artificial intelligence is already reshaping your travel experience. From that first spark of inspiration to the moment we reclaim our luggage at journey's end, AI increasingly operates behind the scenes of travel[9] Today's travellers may barely notice these systems – no visible droids or talking robots – but the apps and platforms we use quietly gather data, predict needs, and personalize our trips. In essence, an ambient or "invisible" intelligence has emerged, one that "analyses data, predicts needs, and delivers personalized experiences without disrupting daily activities"[13]. This new travel landscape spans all corners of the world and every style of journey – leisure vacations, business trips, eco- tours, luxury escapes – and it unfolds from the very first search to the post-trip follow-up.

---

[*] Joshua Lau holds an Executive MBA (Distinction) from the University of Oxford. With work experience across the UK, Japan, China, and Singapore, he combines academic expertise and leadership in business development, government, and academia, focusing on responsible AI in the modern workplace. He works as the Head of Business Development at digital signage company Vieunite in the UK

DOI: 10.1201/9781003737803-4

Planning Ahead: The AI-Powered Itinerary

Imagine yourself sitting at home, sketching a vague plan for a holiday. Instead of hours of browsing, AI-based tools take the reins. They begin by analysing your profile: past trips, budget, stated preferences, even social media likes. These algorithms are “at the forefront of making travel planning seamless and tailored to each traveller’s needs”[4]. For example, corporate clients like Arrivia point out that AI can determine preferences (destinations, budgets, habits), personalize recommendations (hotels, flights, activities), and even create dynamic itineraries that adjust in real time for delays or weather[1]. In practice, this might mean the system remembers you prefer beach hotels over city centers, or that you always travel with a pet, and then instantly customizes search results accordingly. AI can even auto-update your plan; if a storm closes a road on the morning of your trip, the itinerary could re-route itself around the delay without you lifting a finger.

- **Determining Traveller Preferences**: Algorithms mine your data (past trips, budgets, web searches) to infer what kind of trip you want[10].
- **Personalized Recommendations**: The system suggests hotels, flights, or excursions uniquely suited to you – not just the most popular options.
- **Dynamic Itineraries**: Even after you book, AI keeps an eye on your schedule and adapts it. If a flight is cancelled or a concert is unexpectedly on, your plan updates in real time.

By treating each traveller as unique, these tools turn generic vacation ideas into curated "preference-driven adventures"[1]. Indeed, real-world services are already doing this. Trip planning giants have embedded generative chatbots: for instance, Expedia[7] now offers a ChatGPT-powered chat in its app that lets loyalty program members simply "engage in open-ended conversations" to get customized travel advice. Instead of filling forms, you can literally ask the app, "Give me a week-long art-centric Italy itinerary under $3,000" and receive a coherent, detailed plan. Kayak[5] similarly added ChatGPT to its "Best Time to Travel" tool, which analyzes weather, events, and price trends to recommend the cheapest months to visit a destination. These systems don't just fetch data; they compose it. A recent survey found that by March 2024, 41% of North American travellers had already tried generative AI for trip ideas or itineraries, up from 34% just a few months earlier[2]. One user reported that after entering her family's ages and interests, the AI returned "a well-structured day-by-day itinerary with experiences tailored for both kids and adults" – far faster than the hours she previously spent sifting through guidebooks[3].

AI even lets travellers preview destinations in new ways. Virtual reality and AI-generated tours can give an immersive "try-before-you-buy" glimpse of a hotel suite or a mountain trail[10]. Smart search tools can show you photos, maps, and narrative highlights of places you might never otherwise find. Altogether, the pre-trip phase has become a conversation with an intelligent travel designer rather than a chore. Instead of blindly scrolling hundreds of search results, travellers get hyper-personalized inspiration, as if a personal travel agent were doing the legwork. As one industry summary notes, generative AI allows apps to process "vast amounts of data and generate content in real time," delivering custom itineraries, interactive virtual tours, and unique recommendations that make each journey feel personally crafted[10].

A Smart Companion on the Road

Boarding a flight or hopping on a train used to mean fending for oneself amid the chaos of terminals. These days, many travellers have an AI co-pilot in their pocket. Mobile apps now use your location and habits to proactively assist. For example, Trip.com's TripGenie assistant (popular in Asia) has evolved into a "context-aware travel companion"[14]. It knows where you are – literally – and can pop up timely suggestions without even being asked. If you're waiting at a train station, TripGenie might suggest nearby attractions or restaurants; if you're scanning a menu in a foreign language, its visual recognition translates it instantly. Live voice translation features have also appeared – a built-in system can now carry out "speak-and- translate" conversations in real time across a dozen languages. In short, the app "no longer [just responds] to user queries," but anticipates them by tapping into location, browsing history and on-board sensors.

Trip.com's AI travel assistant (shown on smartphone) now personalizes suggestions by knowing where you are and what you've done. The app can auto-translate signs or propose nearby activities, even before you ask.

Beyond TripGenie, mainstream platforms are adding similar helpers. Chatbots now handle airline rebookings and travel advice. Lufthansa, for instance, advertises a Facebook chatbot that can manage irregularities, flight status queries, and baggage issues. Its role is to automate answers that used to require airline support lines. KLM and Emirates have similar social-media assistants (on platforms like Twitter and WhatsApp) for flight updates and customer service. In the airport lounge or on board a plane, these systems quietly collect data: your ticket details, past itineraries, even Wi-Fi connection patterns. Then they forecast problems (like imminent delays or lost bags) and gently nudge you via alerts[11].

Meanwhile, consumer apps like Google Maps and Apple Wallet are getting smarter: they now surface boarding passes and itinerary alerts automatically. A travel app might ping you that your gate has changed or that a nearby lounge has Wi-Fi (based on AI-driven insights). Companies are also using AI to predict and optimize the travel crowding. For example, as an agentic AI future scenario suggests, in-seat devices or wearables could signal your stress or health, prompting an AI to book you a spa break or quieter route. Even if such features are nascent, the trend is clear: AI assistants will inform you before you think to ask, making the journey smoother.

Across travel modes – planes, trains, buses – predictive algorithms help too. Flight apps show fare trends so you know if you should "buy now or wait" (popularized by companies like Hopper). Conference travellers using business apps benefit from AI that syncs flights with calendars and expense reports. Though not glamorous, these quiet optimizations (reducing idle time, cutting ticket costs) represent big gains for time- pressed professionals.

Personalized Stays and Local Experiences

After arrival, AI continues to shape the adventure in hotels, restaurants, and tours. Many hospitality brands already deploy AI-powered concierges. Hilton's famous "Connie" (a Watson AI robot) offers dining and activity tips, while Marriott's chatbots interact via apps and messaging to give loyalty members instant responses. A recent summary notes that chains like Hilton, Marriott and even gaming resort parades now boast AI assistants: the industry is using bots to "streamline the booking process" and handle everything from reservations to bag tracking[3]. In practice, this might mean sending a quick text to the hotel's app saying, "recommend a spa service" and getting back personalized suggestions.

In-room experiences are also getting smarter. Hotels increasingly offer voice-activated room controls (lights, blinds, media) and IoT gadgets that "learn" your preferences (favourite temperature, news channel). Some luxury suites come with built-in tablets or smart mirrors that speak to travel AI: imagine waking up and asking your mirror for today's schedule, or having it suggest a local cafe via image search on the fly. These features are subtle enhancements that rarely disrupt the guest – a gentle voice prompt or notification – yet they knit the stay into a cohesive experience.

On the ground, translation tools bridge language gaps effortlessly. Imagine pointing your phone at a street sign in Tokyo and having it overlay an English translation instantly. Modern AI "menu assistants" can identify foreign text and convert it to speech in real time[8]. Tourists can also benefit from AI-driven guides: apps can use your preferences (art museums vs outdoor markets) to recommend an itinerary for the day. Some advanced platforms even promise dynamic audio tours that adapt to your pace and interests, possibly using augmented reality to overlay historical facts as you look through your camera. For travellers craving novelty, AI can surface hidden gems – less-trafficked parks, a family-run eatery – that match your profile, rather than just pointing you to the mainstream attractions.

Travellers concerned about sustainability are finding AI allies too. Recent studies on eco-tourism highlight that AI can "optimize resource management, monitor biodiversity, [and] enhance visitor experience" in natural parks. In concrete terms, an AI itinerary might suggest a low-emission travel route between sites, or recommend locally owned eco-lodges, reducing carbon and boosting the local economy. Tour operators use AI to predict and smooth out peak crowds at popular destinations (for example, adjusting booking windows to avoid overcapacity). Even online booking engines can flag greener options by default, nudging travellers toward trains instead of short-haul flights. In this way, AI subtly encourages more sustainable choices without requiring travellers to sacrifice convenience.

At the luxury end, AI's role is to make indulgence even more effortless. Luxury travel reports note that today's high-end clients expect personalization and are willing to pay extra for it. For such travellers, AI acts like a 24/7 personal concierge. Imagine you mention in passing that you love jazz music; generative AI could then coordinate with your hotel to schedule a private jazz brunch, or reserve premium concert tickets – without a human ever picking up the phone. One industry commentator observes that an AI travel agent "can effortlessly curate unique recommendations and an itinerary to match, saving travellers time and money". In many ways, technology now allows luxury hotels and tour companies to scale true personalization: the brand still handles the fancy villas and yachts, but an AI helps manage the details tailored to your tastes[6].

Whether it's a backpacker or a billionaire, the result is the same: travel experiences feel more personal and less like cookie-cutter packages. Hotels already track your stay preferences (room type, dining choices) and use machine learning to suggest perks or upgrades you'll enjoy. After check-out, that data feeds into loyalty apps that send you offers for your next trip – for example, an algorithm might notice you always rent a hybrid car and thus email you hybrid-only rental deals for future bookings. The integration is largely invisible but increasingly sophisticated.

Reflection and Loyalty: Post-Trip Personalization

The journey doesn't truly end at home; AI continues working even after you return. Feedback forms and online reviews are now often analyzed by AI to improve services. Some companies automatically parse guest comments to fix issues or spotlight staff for praise – a quiet form of aftercare. On a more personal level, travel apps can compile digital scrapbooks of your trip using AI to organize photos by location and theme. Future tools might even auto-generate a highlight reel of your vacation to share with friends, or suggest future trips based on places you loved most[2].

In the loyalty realm, AI tailors' future offers. For example, Arrivia highlights that airlines and hotel chains use data-driven personalization to strengthen loyalty programs[1]. If you frequently visit Tokyo, your preferred airline knows to offer you insider recommendations on a smaller local brand that big tourists miss. After a trip, they might surprise you with a thank-you note mentioning a museum you loved (an AI noticed you spent extra time there). Over time, the data creates a profile that feels almost like a personal travel agent who "knows your dream destination" and even "anticipates your culinary tastes". In short, AI helps make the end of one trip the start of the next journey – all woven together by personalized follow-ups and targeted deals.

On the Horizon: Agentic AI and New Frontiers

What comes next? Analysts foresee a rise of agentic AI – fully autonomous travel agents that negotiate and act on your behalf. Already, AI can scour tens of thousands of trip options in seconds; soon it may even handle entire bookings end-to-end. Imagine an AI that not only plans your itinerary but executes it: it books flights when prices hit the right level, checks you into hotels, and even coordinates reimbursements without your involvement. A recent analysis suggests that these agentic systems "will act as an expert curator of experiences in real time," optimizing your plan on the fly. For instance, an AI could monitor local traffic and weather during your trip and reroute you to avoid congestion or make up time – all without a human prompting it[15].

In the not-too-distant future, virtual travel agents will fuse all your personal data (preferences, mood, habits) into one omniscient concierge. As one report puts it, an agentic AI will "not only know your dream destination but also anticipate your culinary tastes, accommodation preferences, and even your mood and the weather conditions". This means every step of the trip could be hyper-personalized: the AI might suggest a tranquil afternoon museum visit if it detects you're feeling tired or swap an itinerary slot if it learns you need a break. Although such capabilities raise questions about privacy, they promise a travel experience where the AI's role is to "democratize access to information," surfacing hidden gems that were once hard to find[14].

What is certain is that travellers will come to expect this level of service. Just as Netflix's AI-recommended shows have become the norm in entertainment, future travellers may find anything less than contextual, pro-active travel assistance simply unacceptable[12]. The current "pilot light" of AI in travel is steadily growing into a full engine – one that will quietly drive vacations, business trips, and adventures yet to be imagined.

References

1. Arrivia. (2025). AI and Personalized Travel: Unique Member Journeys. Retrieved from https://www.arrivia.com/insights/ai-personalization-for-unique-member-journeys/

2. Aquent. (2024). How AI and Tech Are Shaping Luxury Travel Experiences. Retrieved from https://aquent.com/blog/how-ai-and-tech-are-shaping-luxury-travel-experiences

3. Covasant. (2025, March 28). How AI-powered Chatbots are revolutionizing customer service in travel and hospitality. Retrieved from https://www.covasant.com/blogs/how-ai-powered-chatbots-are-revolutionizing-customer-service-in-travel-and-hospitality

4. GroMatix. (2024, September 25). AI-Powered Eco-Tourism: A Path to Sustainability. LinkedIn. Retrieved from https://www.linkedin.com/pulse/ai-powered-eco-tourism-path-sustainability-gromatix-2b4tc

5. Kayak. (2023, December 7). Kayak harnesses ChatGPT to advise on best time to travel. GlobeTrender. Retrieved from https://globetrender.com/2023/12/07/kayak-employs-chatgpt-travel- recommendations/

6. Lufthansa Group. (2024). New Lufthansa Digital Services. Retrieved from https://www.lufthansa.com/us/en/new-digital-services

7. Medium – N. Locallens. (2025, June). How Gen AI Became My Travel Companion During Our Family Holiday. Retrieved from https://medium.com/@niralocallens/how-gen-ai-became-my-travel- companion-during-our-family-holiday-0e5c0587f6c2

8. Oliver Wyman. (2024, May). This Is How Generative AI Is Making Travel Planning Easier. Retrieved from https://www.oliverwyman.com/our-expertise/insights/2024/may/generative-ai-leisure-travel-planning-and-inspiration.html

9. Papandreou, T. (2024, August 20). AI is transforming travel: it's getting more personal. Forbes. Retrieved from https://www.forbes.com/sites/timothy-papandreou/2024/08/20/ai-is-transforming-travel-its-getting-more-personal/

10. Perez, M. (2024, October 7). How Generative AI Is Revolutionizing the Travel Industry. Smartvel. Retrieved from https://www.smartvel.com/resources/blog/how-generative-ai-is-revolutionizing-the-travel-industry

11. Sentisight (Neurotechnology). (2022). AI-Powered Travel Planning with Modern Tripadvisor Tool. Retrieved from https://www.sentisight.ai/ai-powered-travel-planning-with-modern-tripadvisor-tool/

12. Stoltz, C. (2025, May 2). I Tried 4 AI Travel Planning Apps. Did Any of Them Actually Make Booking a Trip Easier? AFAR Magazine. Retrieved from https://www.afar.com/magazine/we-tested-ai-travel-planning-apps-here-are-the-3-that-actually-worked

13. StatusNeo. (2023, March 7). Ambient Invisible Intelligence: The Future of AI Integration. Retrieved from https://statusneo.com/ambient-invisible-intelligence-the-future-of-ai-integration/

14. Travel & Tour World. (2025, January 26). How Artificial Intelligence is Revolutionizing the Travel Industry with Personalized Experiences, Dynamic Pricing, and Smart Assistants. Retrieved from https://www.travelandtourworld.com/news/article/how-artificial-intelligence-is-revolutionizing-the-travel-industry-with-personalized-experiences-dynamic-pricing-and-smart-assistants/

15. TravelDailyNews. (2025, May 22). Agentic AI is silently transforming the travel and leisure industries. Retrieved from https://www.traveldailynews.com/column/articles/agentic-ai-is-silently-transforming- the-travel-and-leisure-industries/

Harvesting the Stars

By Partho S. Ghosh*

Introduction: Power from Above

It has been a long time since we began searching for alternative sources of clean energy to address the long-standing global energy crisis[15]. We have made advancements in extracting usable energy from wind, tides, solar rays, biomass, and more.[28] Another important area of focus is reducing the carbon footprint of various processes carried out by humans under the banner of advancing technology and creating future-ready solutions for humanity. Some speak of achieving net-zero carbon emissions, while the more feasible approach of carbon-neutral emissions appears to make greater sense[32].

That being said, regardless of the technology, we have predominantly relied on Earth-based resources for building infrastructure and collecting energy. But what about space?

---

*. Partho S. Ghosh, an accomplished aerospace engineer with a master's in information technology, brings over a decade of space sector expertise, pioneering AI/ML-driven STEM research and inspiring the next generation as a dedicated mentor.

DOI: 10.1201/9781003737803-5

We have all seen and used rooftop solar panels for many years now. The technology is simple: incident solar rays fall on panels made of photovoltaic cells, which convert solar energy into electrical energy. This energy is then distributed to households and industrial power supplies. But what if we could capture this solar energy in space, transmit it to Earth, and finally distribute it through existing power grids? Sounds interesting, right? This is the simplest understanding of space-based solar power[10].

The logical question that arises is: why space-based solar power when we already have well-proven, ground-based solar power systems? Space-based solar power may sound like something straight out of a science fiction movie. Imagine a large solar farm, the size of a square kilometer, in space at an altitude of 36,000 km, orbiting the Earth. This enormous sheet of photovoltaics would continuously receive unlimited energy from our very own Sun, which could then be transmitted back to Earth. Finally, the energy received on Earth would be fed into existing power grids.[10]

Now, think about the complexities involved in each phase of this mega mission – the challenges of designing the components necessary to achieve the required functionalities in each stage, all while working within technical requirements and existing constraints. How would we achieve wireless power transmission? Does this mean that the future may not require wires for transmitting power? Imagine sitting in a room while your electronic device charges automatically without being plugged into any power source, just like Wi-Fi. Is this even possible?

Researchers have already explored this concept in theory and have conducted multiple practical demonstrations at different scales. Yes, space-based solar power still requires considerable work before it can be commercialized. However, in theory, it is not a new concept. So why now? Because we finally have all the key components needed to make it happen. The challenge lies in integrating these components, so they function together in a robust and effective manner. Moreover, the advent of AI – especially in the fields of swarm optimization, computer vision, and natural language understanding – could prove to be the secret ingredient needed to turn this mammoth dream into a revolutionary pursuit of excellence.

Why Space based solar power? Why not just solar panels on Earth?

Solar-powered homes and offices are now commonplace[16]. What began as a trend and a futuristic solution to the ongoing energy crisis has become the first go-to option whenever we speak of green and clean energy. A typical solar installation involves a metallic frame mounted on a rigid surface, on which the solar panel – containing photovoltaic cells – is fixed. There are two main variants: stationary panels and sun trackers. The stationary type operates at maximum output only when the incident sunlight is at its highest intensity, typically for 3–4 hours on a normal sunny day. Sun trackers, as the name suggests, follow the direction of the sunlight. This increases the solar energy collection window by a modest margin[25]. However, both variants are ineffective at night when there is no sunlight, and their efficiency drops significantly during winter and monsoon seasons.

Harvesting solar energy in space directly addresses these limitations of Earth-based solar power[10]. Since solar farms in space are far above the Earth's atmosphere, they are unaffected by seasonal variations. This means their solar panels can receive consistent sunlight all year round, as there are no clouds. Additionally, there is no day–night cycle because the panels can be dynamically oriented to face the Sun at all times. This solves the 3–4 hour peak sunlight limitation faced by Earth-based solar power (EBSP). Furthermore, as per solar experts, the intensity of sunlight in space is almost 8–10 times higher than that received by rooftop solar panels on Earth. But does this mean that space-based solar power (SBSP) would generate 8–10 times more electricity for the same solar energy input? Not quite – the answer is a definite no, and we will discuss the basic technicalities in the next section.

While SBSP may not be an economically viable solution right now, its collective contribution to the global energy landscape could be significant in the decades to come. In the future, no single energy source will operate in isolation; instead, each will have its rightful share in ensuring the sustained availability of energy across diverse geographic locations[12]. A detailed evaluation and continuous monitoring of region-specific energy requirements – alongside the balanced distribution of conventional and non-conventional sources – will be essential for designing the blueprint of the future[23]. This holistic approach will address the global energy challenge in its truest spirit.

The building blocks of SBSP

Complete realization of the SBSP concept for commercial global usage is a highly complex task. This revolutionary project involves four major sub-projects that must each deliver flawlessly if we are to successfully harness energy from our Sun. These sub-projects may be named: *collection, transmission, reception*, and *distribution*. The collection and transmission phase relies on the successful demonstration of solar power satellites (SPS). The reception phase depends on the effective operation of ground-based receivers, or rectifying antennas. Finally, the distribution phase requires compatibility between the reception output and the existing electrical grid infrastructure, specific to each geographical location[10].

SPS can be thought of as an automated solar factory on steroids. The collection phase involves a massive solar farm consisting of thousands of solar panels, surrounded by large optical reflectors[30]. These collect huge amounts of incident solar radiation, which is then efficiently converted into electrical energy at the semiconductor junctions within the photovoltaic cells. The theoretical conversion efficiency depends on the chosen material and the number of junctions. For silicon-based crystalline solar panels, efficiencies could reach up to 30%. You can think of the junction as the point where energy is absorbed before being converted into electrical energy. This energy is then passed on to the transmission system, which consists of a motorized transmission antenna. This antenna can be directed to a user-defined location where the ground receptors are positioned. Typical transmission frequencies would be similar to Wi-Fi, around 2.4 GHz.

Why convert solar energy into electrical energy and then transmit it? Why not directly transmit the captured solar energy? The reason lies in atmospheric absorption: losses are much higher for optical signals (such as visible and UV light) compared to the microwave spectrum. By converting the solar energy into electrical energy first, it can then be effectively transmitted using a microwave carrier frequency. Another viable beaming technique is the use of lasers, which offer high coherence over long distances.

The ground receptors are known as rectifying antennas, or rectennas. Their job is to convert incoming microwave energy into DC electrical energy[3]. This energy is then transmitted via wires to local energy grids for distribution. Selecting rectenna sites is a challenging task due to the large area requirements – often in the range of 5–6 square kilometers. Rectennas may be configured as patch antennas or meshed grids. The expected base output of an SPS is on the order of gigawatts. This raises the question: would directing such a large amount of energy to one location harm biodiversity or the environment?

According to solar energy experts, the effective energy intensity at the rectenna site would be roughly equivalent to one-quarter of normal daylight sun, after accounting for all the conversion losses in the SBSP chain.

The conversion process involves multiple stages:

1. From incident solar energy in space to electrical energy.
2. From electrical energy to microwave energy.
3. Transmission of microwave energy through space and the atmosphere, with associated propagation losses.
4. From received microwave energy back to electrical energy at the rectenna.
5. From DC electrical energy to local grid-compatible power.

The overall conversion efficiency and the losses at each stage will ultimately determine the feasibility and economic viability of SBSP in the years to come[10].

What if we directly transmitted sunlight from space back to Earth? A similar idea has been demonstrated by a company called Reflect Orbital. Their plan is to position huge reflective surfaces (mirrors) in space, orient them toward specific ground locations, and provide artificial sunlight during the darkest nights at those locations. Sounds fascinating, doesn't it?

The role of AI in making SBSP possible

Having understood the fundamentals, the driving technologies, and the associated challenges, it becomes imperative to take a novel approach if we are to realize SBSP in its true spirit. Artificial intelligence will play an irreplaceable role in the end-to-end execution of this complex mission – whether it is setting up SPS, orienting solar panels for optimal incident radiation, selecting rectenna sites, performing grid compatibility studies, monitoring all segments of SBSP, and much more[1]. The list is virtually endless.

Setting up kilometer-wide solar farms at geostationary altitudes is an immensely complex task[10]. Consider this: thousands of space missions would be required just to transport the necessary solar panels into orbit, as each launch vehicle has a limited payload capacity. Once in position, these panels would need to be aligned, oriented, and connected to one another in a precise manner, both mechanically and electrically. Achieving this would require a fully functional robotic swarm[9,34] operating in outer space, with each robot responsible for carrying and managing a single solar panel. To make this possible, robust computer vision algorithm is essential, as real-time feedback from ground control may not be feasible in such scenarios.

It is now clear that traditional human monitoring alone would not suffice for the SBSP mission. However, the human element and feedback remain vital at every phase. All machine learning predictions – whether related to solar panel orientations, global power surges and demands, or grid integration – must be validated at regular intervals. While real-time evaluation of computer vision tasks may be impractical, scheduled monitoring of solar farm configurations, drafting of damage mitigation plans, and execution of sustained maintenance tasks will require human intervention.[1]

Thus, a balanced combination of human expertise and the power of AI is the key to realizing a global-scale SBSP solution.

AI in satellite positioning and solar array orientation

Knowing where the Sun will shine and at what time is the key to harnessing the maximum incident solar energy. On Earth, a sun tracker is fixed at a particular location, and tracking is achieved by re-orienting the solar panels. Compare this to a solar panel within a solar farm in an SPS. What is the difference? For starters, the solar panels in an SPS number in the thousands. They are part of a massive solar farm and float freely in space, without rigid mounting. This means we must first position the SPS itself and then re-orient the individual solar panels to collect the maximum incident solar radiation[11].

On Earth, we already have solar insolation data at the surface. For SPS, the same type of data is required for all times of the day and throughout the year, but at geostationary altitudes. Using this data, we can train a machine learning model to predict the required positions of individual solar panels, based on their relative configurations within the solar farm and the Sun's tracked position. The model would also predict the specific orientations of the panels. Here, *position* refers to the three translations along the X, Y, and Z axes, while orientation refers to the three rotations about the X, Y, and Z axes, respectively.

Tracking the Sun's position in real time and dynamically adjusting the positions and orientations of the panels helps maximize energy output[11]. The solar farm in an SPS can be thought of as a collection of numerous solar arrays, each consisting of many panels. Surrounding these arrays is a wall of large optical reflectors (mirrors). Imagine the solar farm as a football field, with the massive mirrors forming curved walls around it. Artificial intelligence would play a vital role in positioning the SPS, re-orienting the solar arrays, and adjusting the reflectors to achieve maximum solar energy collection.

Thus, the collection project, as discussed in the building blocks of SBSP, heavily relies on robust machine learning algorithms to achieve its full functionality.

AI in wireless power transmission

Wireless power transmission (WPT) is at the heart of the SBSP mission. While the collection, reception, and distribution phases fall within the traditional wired power transfer framework, the transmission phase relies solely on WPT. Simply put, it means transferring power from point A to point B without physical cables[14]. However, a carrier is required, and the choice of carrier must minimize transmission losses. As discussed, there are two main options: microwaves and lasers.

Fundamentally, both microwaves and lasers are part of the electromagnetic spectrum, operating at different frequencies. We require electromagnetic radiation (EMR) as a carrier for WPT because there is no physical medium in space. An EMR consists of orthogonally oscillating electric and magnetic fields. The higher the frequency, the greater the energy loss (attenuation) due to atmospheric absorption. Microwaves typically operate at $\sim 10^{12}$ Hz, while visible light in lasers operates at $\sim 10^{15}$ Hz. This explains why microwaves are preferred over lasers for WPT from SPS to ground rectennae.

How do we steer a microwave beam in the desired direction? One approach is to mechanically rotate the antenna about the tip and tilt axes using a motor. This method works for helical antennas or horn antennas. But what if we use a patch array antenna?[17] This is where electronic beam steering comes into play.

Imagine ten microwave sources arranged in a straight line on a patch antenna (visualize it as a flat board). If all sources are powered simultaneously with the same intensity, the result is a strong beam focused in one direction. Now, consider powering the sources at slightly different times, introducing a controlled phase difference between adjacent sources. Although each source completes a full power cycle (from zero to maximum, down to minimum, and back to zero), in tandem they produce a beam that steers from left to right, depending on the timing of the sources. This achieves electronic steering about one axis (say, the tip axis). Similarly, by arranging another set of microwave sources vertically (top to bottom of the patch antenna), we can achieve steering about the tilt axis. Together, this enables tip-tilt electronic beam steering. Artificial intelligence assists in predicting the precise beam alignment required for maximum energy transfer to the ground rectenna, based on atmospheric models and real-time weather conditions.

Numerical weather prediction models heavily leverage machine learning to make informed forecasts about atmospheric conditions[7]. This data serves as a real-time guide for planning beam power levels and steering operations on board the SPS, thereby enabling efficient WPT through Earth's atmosphere. Additionally, these models help predict safe transmission levels, accounting for biodiversity at the beaming location. Thus, AI ensures both efficiency and safety in the WPT process by providing intelligent controls and fail-safes.

AI for ground reception and grid integration

After exploring the use of AI in the collection and transmission phases, we now focus on the remaining two phases: reception and distribution. The reception station comprises a well-structured farm of receiving antennas, spanning an area of 5–6 sq. km. RF-to-DC conversion efficiency is the key metric that must be optimized for a given rectenna configuration[3]. To understand the underlying technical principles, a graduate-level understanding of antenna theory and basic electronics is sufficient. AI can provide better control over the design and operational parameters of rectenna elements such as the rectifier and impedance matching networks[27].

Why is this important?

Impedance is the net opposition to the flow of electrical current in any circuit. It is constituted by the resistance offered by resistive elements and the reactance offered by capacitive and inductive elements. The receiving antenna, antenna feed, and rectifying electronics must be impedance-matched to minimize overall losses[20,21]. The incoming RF beam carries harnessed solar energy in the form of electrical energy. A receiving antenna converts the RF into electrical energy, and a rectifier then converts the AC output into DC. Hence the name: rectenna.

Predictive, proactive maintenance of rectenna elements using computer vision and machine learning can help monitor, identify, and prevent component failures. Dedicated machine learning models may also be used to monitor resource utilization, predict surges in power demand at specific geographic locations, and accordingly command the SPS to alter the intensity of transmitted microwave beams. All of this can be monitored at scheduled intervals by a qualified technician. This ensures a human-in-the-loop approach to reviewing the policy decisions made by AI algorithms in SBSP operations.

Operational load-balancing algorithms already exist in our local grids. The challenge lies in distributing SBSP energy into these grids[5]. AI prediction models can play a significant role in ensuring compatibility between the rectenna network and the electrical grid network. Overloads in any part of the grid can be predicted and prevented using the insights collected[33]. If overlooked, uncontrolled overloads can result in partial or complete regional blackouts and severely damage the electrical loads connected to both industrial and residential sub-grids. Over-voltage, over-current, and short circuits are all possible consequences of such overloads. And the downtime? It can range from hours to days – and in some cases, even months.

Simulation, Digital twins and Autonomous operation

Now that we have a good understanding of what SBSP is all about and the role of AI in making it better, can we start realizing it? Not really. We need to begin with the basics. Yes, we already possess the necessary technology, more of which will be discussed in the next section. However, our first step is to simulate a working SBSP model. Just like the real mission, this will be divided into four projects. The specifications and constraints of all four phases should be clearly listed and understood before we begin designing the simulation. We must always take note of the scope, assumptions, and limitations of a simulated environment. While the AI models used will be the same (or early versions) as those intended for the real mission, the key missing components are the physical hardware and accurate environmental conditions.

We begin by creating a digital twin for both the SPS and the ground station. This involves a detailed hierarchical breakdown of the components, subsystems, and systems that make up an SPS and a ground station. The scope, assumptions, and limitations will play a vital role in bridging the gaps in digital twin creation. End-to-end data pipelines will be the backbone of these digital twins, ensuring their effectiveness. These pipelines will include a clear definition of data sources, preprocessing steps, component interactions, subsystem-level handshakes, desired outputs, predictions, evaluation, ranking, and constructive feedback. AI will be seamlessly integrated within these digital twins, which will then be used to simulate the four predefined phases[13].

Speaking of the gap between simulation and the real world, space environments are hostile on many fronts. The systems on board the SPS must withstand extreme temperatures, vacuum, and radiation events. Deep space temperatures are around 4K, whereas the maximum temperature experienced by the solar farm could reach ~400K. Radiation events such as single-event upsets and low-resistance path latch-ups can damage on-board electronics. While radiation-hardened electronics are the preferred approach, radiation-tolerant systems are often a feasible alternative. That being said, we must set up, align, and operate massive optical reflectors and kilometer-wide solar farms in such environments. This makes autonomous robotic swarms for solar farm setup in space a well-known challenge. What complicates matters further is that simulating exact conditions – particularly radiation exposure and weak or absent communication signals at different locations – is extremely difficult. Hardware-in-the-loop testing is therefore necessary to validate the flightworthiness of our claims regarding the robustness of any automation system envisioned for the SBSP mission.

Progress so far: From prototypes to proposals

So, where is the world right now in the SBSP context? As mentioned in the introductory section, the baseline concept of space-based solar power is not new. Similarly, wireless power transmission (WPT) has been known for ages, dating back to the time of Nikola Tesla. In fact, NASA demonstrated a WPT of 36 kW across a designated distance in 1976. Almost half a century has passed since then. Focused research on the various domains necessary to realize SBSP was carried out by NASA in the late 1980s and early 1990s. Although a complete description is beyond the scope of this chapter, the interested reader can certainly search for *SBSP studies done in the recent past*.

With similar dedication, China and Japan have made considerable advancements in this field. In fact, China has already demonstrated a milliwatt-level WPT from space to ground and has proposed a step-by-step roadmap for the next decade to achieve watt-level, kilowatt-level, and megawatt-level WPT using its own SPS. Ambitious, isn't it?

Quite recently, a group of US researchers demonstrated WPT from space using origami-inspired solar films (also called *solar carpets*). The team worked on this for almost a decade and successfully incorporated the entire photovoltaic circuit within a thickness on the order of tens of microns. Similar research on ultra-thin solar films with nearly 45% conversion efficiency has also been achieved by a focused MIT group. What's next?

A company named Space Solar has made commendable strides in developing and testing different systems needed to realize SBSP. Another US-based company has demonstrated and commercialized WPT for charging household devices like phones, tablets, and even drones located within the same room. Some private players are also working on thin-film technologies that would aid in the creation of lightweight solar panels. While private sector participation is on the rise, a commonly agreed-upon directive is necessary to streamline efforts, much like government-led initiatives.

This goes to show that, technologically, we already have much of what is needed to achieve full-scale SBSP[4,6]. Then what's stopping us? Economic viability, governmental support, community acceptance, and most important of all – a belief that SBSP could be the solution to complement our future clean and green energy needs[22]. Currently, Earth-based solar power (EBSP) is far more economical than SBSP. The general preference is to install greater numbers of solar panels at locations receiving high-intensity solar radiation. China has taken this a step further – covering an entire mountain with solar panels!

If we are to work toward making SBSP a viable option, we need to focus on two things: reducing launch costs and reducing manufacturing costs. Reusable launch vehicles are the answer to the first problem, and in-space manufacturing[8] is the answer to the second. While past in-space manufacturing experiments have been carried out onboard the ISS, this remains an underexplored area – especially micro-level additive manufacturing in microgravity conditions[18]. Current research focuses on in-situ resource utilization to manufacture macro-scale components in space. Deep space mining, such as the Artemis mission and asteroid mining, is aligned with this vision.

SBSP-related work is in progress, but much more needs to be done. The interested reader may refer to a comprehensive 108-page report[24] authored by NASA, which presents an end-to-end blueprint of an SBSP mission, including technical details, budget requirements, business plans, and much more. The report explores two variant configurations for the mission and emphasizes the two major problems that need to be addressed.

The road ahead: What more is needed?

We have seen what has been achieved so far in SBSP, and we have also explored some possible starting points for the much-needed future work. So, are you excited to continue this revolutionary journey? Join the *Space Based Solar Power Community*[26], today!

To begin with, we will target composite self-healing materials for the majority of space structures to be used in SPS.[29] This would help prevent frequent replacements after micrometeoroid impacts and space debris collisions. We will also place ample focus on miniaturizing electronics well beyond the current 30-micron thickness limit for single-junction photovoltaic cells. This limit is dictated by the photon absorption efficiency of the photovoltaic material. Our aim is to scale the 3-micron-thick ultra-thin solar film (10 cm × 10 cm) to the size of a full solar panel for use on board the SBSP[2]. Challenging enough?

We have already discussed the importance of in-space manufacturing. Both macro-scale and micro-scale manufacturing setups need to be designed, tested, validated, and made ready for use long before we build our first SPS. According to NASA, the cost to build the first SPS would be upwards of USD 16 billion, assuming the use of current state-of-the-art technologies. The subsequent SPS units would cost upwards of USD 4 billion each[24]. Do you now appreciate the scale of this multi-billion-dollar SBSP project? Think about its ROI in terms of global energy sufficiency and ensuring a sustained clean and green energy source for decades to come.

Significant advancements in energy storage will also be necessary. While today's focus is on improving EV battery efficiency and developing systematic battery management systems, storage solutions tailored to SBSP are essential. This is because not all collected energy may necessarily be transmitted to the rectenna, and similarly, not all transmitted energy may be immediately distributed. Thus, an efficient energy storage solution is required for both space and ground usage[19]. Ever heard of gravity batteries?

Apart from the technical challenges, there is also a long list of regulatory requirements that must be met. These vary depending on geopolitics, and careful attention will be necessary to avoid bottlenecks in our journey to realize SBSP. Country-specific energy policies must be adhered to in planning the mission. Collaborations such as the International Solar Alliance (ISA) actively support the ideals of net-zero carbon emissions and would be a strong partner for SBSP. In addition, region-specific schemes can be leveraged to accelerate the realization process.

Finally, deep-technology investors should find SBSP an exciting prospect. From an investor's perspective, it may seem like a long shot, as the required risk appetite is enormous. There is absolutely no system heritage, and funding would rely solely on the team's approach, proven competence, ethics, and integrity. As a researcher or business leader, your long-term vision must be crystal clear, as well as the steps needed to achieve it. The ultimate goal is to provide a sustainable, global solution for clean energy through space-based solar power.

Risk, Ethics, and Public Perception

Worried about the environmental and health concerns of SBSP? Won't a focused beam from space be harmful to humans and animals here on Earth? What about its impact on plant life?

Firstly, you are not alone. Anyone who has researched SBSP has surely come across these questions. The answer is short and clear: microwave beams in SBSP are non-ionizing in nature and therefore do not affect the biodiversity in their path. Also, as discussed earlier, the maximum intensity received by the rectenna is only a fourth of that of normal sunlight. Hence, the beaming technique is safe.

Secondly, can these directed beams be used as weapons? In the same configuration, definitely not. With increased intensity, yes, they can. It all depends on whether we use the technology as a boon for the good of society or turn it into a bane with ulterior motives. The choice is ours.

Thirdly, all process pipelines involved in the four projects of SBSP, collection, transmission, reception, and distribution, should include a user-centric explainer of the operating steps. This ensures transparency and builds trust among the general populace.

And lastly, we need to respect the long-term vision of serving the world's energy needs through the realization of SBSP. Therefore, global access with distributed, structured infrastructure and resource control is essential whenever we plan a large-scale commercial rollout.

Conclusion: A dream within reach

It is quite humbling to note that what began as a thought to craft a cleaner, greener, and energy-sufficient tomorrow has now matured by leaps and bounds, rewriting existing stereotypes, venturing into what was once thought impossible, and revolutionizing reality with a boon in the making. Space-based solar power: the potential is endless.

Our task now is to coalesce the best of human intellect with the power of artificial intelligence. This synergy is inevitable and is undoubtedly the way forward to a brighter and smarter tomorrow. That said, we as humans must work toward ensuring the ethical, responsible, and explainable use of AI in everything we apply it to. Our future will thank us later!

References

1. Adadi, A., & Berrada, M. (2018). Peeking inside the Black-box: A survey on explainable artificial intelligence (XAI). IEEE Access, 6, 52138-52160. https://doi.org/10.1109/access.2018.2870052
2. Al Suny, A., Sultan, R. B., Tohfa, S., Haque, A. J., & Chowdhury, M. H. (2023). The use of Plasmonic metal nanoparticles to enhance the opto-electronic performance of thin-film/Ultrathin film CdTe solar cells. 2023 International Conference on Electrical, Computer and Communication Engineering (ECCE), 1-6. https://doi.org/10.1109/ecce57851.2023.10101669
3. Alibakhshikenari, M., Virdee, B. S., See, C. H., Abd-Alhameed, R. A., Falcone, F., & Limiti, E. (2020). Energy harvesting circuit with high RF-to-DC conversion efficiency.

2020 IEEE International Symposium on Antennas and Propagation and North American Radio Science Meeting, 1299-1300. https://doi.org/10.1109/ieeeconf35879.2020.9329604

4. Ambatali, C. D., Nakasuka, S., & Miyazaki, Y. (2023). Comparison of different solar cell-antenna integration designs on a thin film space-based solar power station. 2023 17th European Conference on Antennas and Propagation (EuCAP), 1-5. https://doi.org/10.23919/eucap57121.2023.10133507

5. Awaja, N., Holmes, D. G., & Wilkinson, R. H. (2014). Integrating high penetration renewable generation into an electrical grid network. 2014 Australasian Universities Power Engineering Conference (AUPEC), 1-6. https://doi.org/10.1109/aupec.2014.6966639

6. Barde, H. (2023). A power engineer view on space based solar power. 2023 13th European Space Power Conference (ESPC), 1-11. https://doi.org/10.1109/espc59009.2023.10298124

7. Bauer, P., Thorpe, A., & Brunet, G. (2015). The quiet revolution of numerical weather prediction. Nature, 525(7567), 47-55. https://doi.org/10.1038/nature14956

8. Bhundiya, H. G., Royer, F., & Cordero, Z. (2022). Engineering framework for assessing materials and processes for in-space manufacturing. Journal of Materials Engineering and Performance, 31(8), 6045-6059. https://doi.org/10.1007/s11665-022-06755-y

9. Cai, W., Liu, Z., Zhang, M., & Wang, C. (2023). Cooperative artificial intelligence for underwater robotic swarm. Robotics and Autonomous Systems, 164, 104410. https://doi.org/10.1016/j.robot.2023.104410

10. Chowdhury, A. (2023). Method of space based solar power extraction using microwaves. International Journal of Scientific Research in Engineering and Management, 07(07). https://doi.org/10.55041/ijsrem24349

11. Colagrossi, A., & Lavagna, M. (2022). A spacecraft attitude determination and control algorithm for solar arrays pointing leveraging sun angle and angular rates measurements. Algorithms, 15(2), 29. https://doi.org/10.3390/a15020029

12. Das, S. S., Kumar, J., Dawn, S., & Salata, F. (2023). Existing stature and possible outlook of renewable power in comprehensive electricity market. Processes, 11(6), 1849. https://doi.org/10.3390/pr11061849

13. Fuller, A., Fan, Z., Day, C., & Barlow, C. (2020). Digital twin: Enabling technologies, challenges and open research. IEEE Access, 8, 108952-108971. https://doi.org/10.1109/access.2020.2998358

14. Gao, J., Zhou, J., Yuan, C., Zhang, Z., Gao, C., Yan, G., Li, R., & Zhang, L. (2023). Stable wireless power transmission for a capsule robot with randomly changing attitude. IEEE Transactions on Power Electronics, 38(2), 2782-2796. https://doi.org/10.1109/tpel.2022.3212699

15. Gielen, D., Boshell, F., Saygin, D., Bazilian, M. D., Wagner, N., & Gorini, R. (2019). The role of renewable energy in the global energy transformation. Energy Strategy Reviews, 24, 38-50. https://doi.org/10.1016/j.esr.2019.01.006

16. Huang, H., & Cheng, L. (2022). Predicting intention of residential solar installation: The role of ecological lifestyle, consumer innovativeness, perceived benefit, government incentives, and solar product knowledge. Energy & Environment, 34(6), 1826-1843. https://doi.org/10.1177/0958305x221100525

17. Jackson, B., Saravanakumar, R., Balachander, B., Haldorai, A., S., V., & A. Sahaya, A. N. (2022). Modified design structure of a metamaterial microstrip patch array antenna for RF energy optimization. Materiali in tehnologije, 56(2). https://doi.org/10.17222/mit.2022.384

18. Kringer, M., Böhrer, C., Frey, M., Pimpi, J., & Pietras, M. (2022). Direct robotic extrusion of photopolymers (DREPP): Influence of microgravity on an in-space manufacturing

method. Frontiers in Space Technologies, 3. https://doi.org/10.3389/frspt.2022.899242

19. Larcher, D., & Tarascon, J. (2015). Towards greener and more sustainable batteries for electrical energy storage. Nature Chemistry, 7(1), 19-29. https://doi.org/10.1038/nchem.2085

20. Lauder, D., & Sun, Y. (2020). Design considerations of antennas and adaptive impedance matching networks for RF energy harvesting. 2020 European Conference on Circuit Theory and Design (ECCTD), 1-4. https://doi.org/10.1109/ecctd49232.2020.9218310

21. Lee, D., Kim, T., Kim, S., Byun, K., & Kwon, K. (2018). A CMOS rectifier with 72.3% RF-to-DC conversion efficiency employing tunable impedance matching network for ambient RF energy harvesting. 2018 International SoC Design Conference (ISOCC). https://doi.org/10.1109/isocc.2018.8649983

22. Malaviya, P., Sarvaiya, V., Shah, A., Thakkar, D., & Shah, M. (2022). A comprehensive review on space solar power satellite: An idiosyncratic approach. Environmental Science and Pollution Research, 29(28), 42476-42492. https://doi.org/10.1007/s11356-022-19560-w

23. Pourasl, H. H., Barenji, R. V., & Khojastehnezhad, V. M. (2023). Solar energy status in the world: A comprehensive review. Energy Reports, 10, 3474-3493. https://doi.org/10.1016/j.egyr.2023.10.022

24. Rodgers, E., Gertsen, E., Sotudeh, J., Mullins, C., Hernandez, A., Le, H. N., Smith, P., & Joseph, N. (2024). Space-Based Solar Power (20230018600). Office of Technology, Policy, and Strategy, NASA. https://www.nasa.gov/wp-content/uploads/2024/01/otps-sbsp-report-final-tagged-approved-1-8-24-tagged-v2.pdf

25. Singh, R., Kumar, S., Gehlot, A., & Pachauri, R. (2018). An imperative role of sun trackers in photovoltaic technology: A review. Renewable and Sustainable Energy Reviews, 82, 3263-3278. https://doi.org/10.1016/j.rser.2017.10.018

26. Space Based Solar Power Community [A focused community for the discussion and dissemination of knowledge and technical updates related to space based solar power research.]. (2025, August). LinkedIn. https://www.linkedin.com/groups/11803388/

27. Surender, D., Halimi, M. A., Khan, T., Talukdar, F. A., Nasimuddin, & Rengarajan, S. R. (2023). 5G/millimeter-wave Rectenna systems for radio-frequency energy harvesting/Wireless power transmission applications: An overview. IEEE Antennas and Propagation Magazine, 65(3), 57-76. https://doi.org/10.1109/map.2022.3208794

28. Twidell, J. (2021). Renewable energy resources (4th ed.). Taylor & Francis. https://doi.org/10.4324/9780429452161

29. Ullah, H., M Azizli, K. A., Man, Z. B., Ismail, M. B., & Khan, M. I. (2016). The potential of Microencapsulated self-healing materials for Microcracks recovery in self-healing composite systems: A review. Polymer Reviews, 56(3), 429-485. https://doi.org/10.1080/15583724.2015.1107098

30. Urdaneta, G. A., Meyers, C., & Rogalski, L. (2022). Solar power satellites: Technical challenges and economic feasibility. Future Energy, 1(2), 9-16. https://doi.org/10.55670/fpll.fuen.1.2.3

31. Visser, H. J. (2020). Radiative wireless energy transfer: Rectifying antennas. Compendium on Electromagnetic Analysis, 219-244. https://doi.org/10.1142/9789813270305_0005

32. Zhang, Y., & Umair, M. (2023). Examining the interconnectedness of green finance: An analysis of dynamic spillover effects among green bonds, renewable energy, and carbon markets. Environmental Science and Pollution Research, 30(31), 77605-77621. https://doi.org/10.1007/s11356-023-27870-w

33. Zhao, Y., Sun, T., & Liu, Y. (2023). Reliability analysis of a loading dependent system with cascading failures considering overloads. Quality and Reliability Engineering

International, 40(3), 1182-1196. https://doi.org/10.1002/qre.3475

34. Zhong, S., Qi, Y., Chen, Z., Wu, J., Chen, H., & Liu, M. (2024). DCL-SLAM: A distributed collaborative LiDAR SLAM framework for a robotic swarm. IEEE Sensors Journal, 24(4), 4786-4797. https://doi.org/10.1109/jsen.2023.3345541

Stamped in Silicon: When Robots Queue at Customs

By Richard R. Khan*

Departure: Gate A23

Introduction: Wheels-Up Questions

Maya tapped her boarding pass against the cool glass of the automated gate while Cal – her carbon-fiber companion – stood beside her, quiet but unmistakably alive with subtle servo hums. A security officer glanced from Maya to the robot's neutral faceplate, eyebrows raised. "Does it... uh... need a passport?" he asked.

Maya smiled. "He's on my travel manifest as equipment."

The gate accepted the scan with a satisfied beep, but the brief exchange left her thinking. If Cal could answer questions, interpret jokes, and even adjust his posture to calm the nervous toddler nearby, was it honest to label him luggage? The line of travelers shuffled forward, and Maya pictured customs on the other side of the Atlantic:

---

* Richard R. Khan is an AI/ML and IT executive with more than 20 years of experience in digital transformation and software engineering, and currently the Vice President of Software Development, driving enterprise AI strategies that cut costs and grow revenues.

DOI: 10.1201/9781003737803-6

stamped books for humans, red-eyed scanners for baggage, and a gray zone where Cal did not quite belong. The very ordinariness of the scene made the underlying puzzle snap into focus – what, exactly, counts as a person in 2025?

The Liminal Companion

Cal carried two internal lithium packs, a multilingual model of large-language AI, and a social-interaction suite that let him track eye contact and match vocal tone. He wasn't built to mimic flesh; his designers chose brushed alloy over synthetic skin, the better to avoid the uncanny valley. Even so, travelers stared. One woman whispered, "Is that the Saudi robot? The one with citizenship?" – proof that a single headline about Sophia in 2017 still rippled through public memory.

Maya had rehearsed her answer for border control: Cal is an assistive device – autonomous but always under my supervision. Yet she knew the admission form's boxes – Are you bringing plants, animals, arms? – were never meant for minds built on silicon.

Defining Personhood

At the heart of Maya's worry sits a centuries-old divide. Natural persons are human beings; legal persons are entities – think corporations or, in New Zealand's case, even a sacred river[1] – granted rights so societies can make sense of accountability. A multinational can own property and sue; a river can be represented in court to prevent pollution. But Cal?

Law professors like Chemerinsky[2] remind students that U.S. courts have inched beyond flesh before – Citizens United extended free-speech protections to firms that exist only on paper. Elsewhere, the European Parliament has floated the idea of electronic personhood for highly autonomous systems[3], a placeholder that lets regulators assign duties – insurance, maintenance logs, update audits – without pretending robots feel joy or pain.

Philosophers add another filter. Descartes said thinking proved existence[4]; Kant tied personhood to the ability to reason about morality[5]; Peter Singer[6] widens the gate to any being that can suffer. Cal passes every cognitive benchmark his engineers devised, but he still lacks subjective experience – or so most scientists insist. The debate feels abstract until you picture an immigration officer holding out a blue passport and Cal extending a polymer hand to take it.

Terminal Conversations

Maya and Cal found two seats near Gate A23. Cal ran a quiet status check – battery 87%, gyros nominal – and turned to Maya.

Cal: "Your heart rate is elevated twenty percent above baseline. Is the upcoming presentation worrying you?"

Maya: "Not the talk. The transit. I keep picturing us stuck at customs."

Cal: "I have reviewed the Schengen regulations on commercial equipment. There is no clause that prohibits an autonomous device from disembarking."

Maya (half-laughing): "Yeah, but there's also no clause that includes you."

Their dialogue – fluid, unscripted – drew a small audience. A teenager asked for a selfie. A flight attendant wondered if Cal could help translate Korean announcements. The robot obliged; his voice pitched low so as not to disturb boarding calls. For a moment Maya watched social norms stretch and restitch around Cal: humans queuing, adjusting, making mental space for a non-human traveler. Cultural adaptation in real time.

Scene Change: Jetway Ethics

Once aboard, Cal folded into seat 12C, torso rigid to comply with safety restraints. The cabin crew briefed Maya on lithium-battery procedures, uncomfortable with the idea that the "device" might decide to stand up mid-flight. She powered his mobility motors down, leaving only conversational subsystems active.

As the aircraft roared down the runway, she scrolled through research notes:

- **Liability puzzles** – If Cal's arm were to knock a hot coffee onto a passenger, would Maya's personal insurance cover it or would the manufacturer be dragged into court?
- **Security concerns** – Advanced robots can be hacked like laptops, yet they occupy physical space beside people. Airports plan drills for lost bags, not compromised exoskeletons.

- **Public perception** – Studies show reactions swing between awe and fear, driven by blockbuster nightmares about machine rebellion.

The questions weren't science-fiction anymore; they were tucked into the safety cards no one reads.

A Thought Experiment at 30,000 Feet

Cal's optics dimmed to night mode while cabin lights faded. Maya pictured two alternate futures:

1. **Robot as Tool** – Cal remains classified as property. Accountability flows through his owner, and any harm he causes routes back to Maya and, by extension, Cal's manufacturer[7]. Regulators relax; insurance underwriters sigh with relief.
2. **Robot as Limited Agent** – Cal holds a thin electronic personhood: he can sign for software updates, carry a digital wallet for in-flight purchases, maybe even hold a biometric travel token. Liability shifts to a mix of robot trust funds and mandatory service logs.

Both futures demand new paperwork at border control – and new social scripts in the aisle of Flight AZ432.

Closing the Day's Chapter

Hours later, land lights glimmered beneath broken cloud. As descent began, Cal whispered, "Maya, I have compiled the entry requirements for devices possessing wireless modules. Would you like me to rehearse them with you?"

Maya nodded, but her mind wandered. Somewhere below, an immigration officer would soon decide whether an articulate machine could step across an invisible line. The officer's rubber stamp might foretell the shape of tomorrow's laws and, by extension, tomorrow's definition of "us."

Checkpoint: Between Worlds

Arrival: Painted Lines and Rubber Stamps

The wheels touched tarmac under a gray Roman dawn. Cabin lights blinked awake as Flight AZ432 rolled to a stop, and Cal re-initialized his motion actuators. Maya's fellow passengers streamed toward the exit, but the purser blocked Cal with a polite hand. "One moment – security will want a word." Maya offered the pre-printed forms: battery documentation, CE-conformity sheet, proof of ownership. Still, an escort arrived to walk the pair down a quieter jet-bridge used for musical instruments and diplomatic pouches – things that fit neither passenger nor cargo. Cal's gyro-stabilized steps matched Maya's, yet every echo of alloy on concrete felt like a courtroom gavel.

At immigration, the glass booth was split: *EU/EEA Citizens, All Passports*, and an improvised lane labeled *Special Items*. A bored officer scanned Cal's QR tag, frown deepening when the data field for citizenship showed *N/A*. "Purpose of visit?" he asked Maya. "Academic conference," she replied, "and he –"

"He?" the officer echoed.

"Cal is demonstration equipment – autonomous but supervised."

The officer's thumb hovered over Refuse Entry. He muttered something about Regolamento 399/2016, the Schengen Borders Code, which never imagined conversational luggage. Maya swallowed; this was the moment abstract philosophy met fluorescent reality.

Customs Dilemma

Across a yellow stripe lay Customs, armed with forms built for laptops and lithium drills. The officer flagged three issues:

1. **Dual-Use Tech** – Cal's encrypted vision module might trigger export-control rules under the EU's Commission Delegated Regulation 2024/67.
2. **Hazardous Batteries** – IATA's guidance treats >100 Wh lithium packs as restricted goods, demanding special declarations and fire-resistant packaging.
3. **Undefined Legal Status** – Autonomous decision-making put Cal outside the "tool" category, yet no field existed for "electronic person."

Maya cited the European Parliament's 2017 resolution proposing electronic personhood for high-autonomy robots. The officer chuckled. "That text isn't binding, signora. Until Rome passes something real, your friend here is just expensive freight."

Yet precedent lurked even in passports: Saudi Arabia's symbolic citizenship for Sophia in 2017 had already cracked the conceptual door. If a state could grant status by decree, could another deny mere entry?

Legal Crossroads

The impasse triggered a tri-phone call – Customs, Border Police, and the Ministry's AI desk. Maya listened as jargon ricocheted: liability matrix, mens rea, third-party risk pools. Under Italian civil code, damage caused by property flows back to the owner, unless "the thing" possesses independent agency. Cal's 32-bit decisions muddied that lineage. Similar puzzles had surfaced after self-driving-car collisions, where courts juggled manufacturer versus operator culpability.

Chemerinsky's lectures on constitutional twilight came to mind: U.S. corporations – mere ink on paper – won free-speech rights in Citizens United (2010). If intangible entities could gain person-like liberties, why not an embodied intelligence? Opponents answer that rights map to moral agency, not processing power. Descartes equated thought with existence, Kant linked dignity to rational will, and Peter Singer widened moral circles to any being that can suffer. Cal, who never felt pain, failed Singer's test; yet he excelled at rational inference, flirting with Kant's. Legal scholars now floated a middle path: grant robots limited agency for contracts and warranty obligations, while reserving human rights for the flesh born.

Ethics on Trial

A slim ethics officer arrived, tablet in hand. "We've no protocol for AI empathy," he sighed, eyeing Cal's powered-down gaze. He posed the trolley-problem classic: "If your algorithm must choose between your safety and mine, which way does the code swing?"

Cal answered softly, "My core directive prioritizes human life over this unit's structural integrity."

Maya held her breath; honesty might invite confiscation for safety review. Instead, the officer nodded as though Cal had passed a parole interview. Ethically aligned design documents – IEEE EAD 2019 – urge such transparent value hierarchies. Yet transparency courts vulnerability: every clear rule is a roadmap for malicious hacks. Airports already worried about cyber-intrusions; a compromised humanoid could bypass both doors and doubt.

The Unofficial Hearing

They shifted to a side room – fluorescent, beige, faint smell of confiscated cheese. Three chairs, one power outlet. Cal's battery ticked down to 76%. The impromptu panel weighed options:

- **Classify Cal as Cargo**. He'd ride freight, gather dust in a warehouse until paperwork cleared. Downside: liability if climate-control failed.
- **Grant Temporary Technical Visa**. A stop-gap card already used for show-cars and film drones. Pros: keeps schedule. Cons: no legal basis for interactive autonomy.
- **Recognize Limited Personhood for 72 hours**. The boldest choice, citing electronic-agent clauses in EU

draft AI Act. It would let Cal sign his own customs bond, with a blockchain escrow for damages.

Maya argued the third path. She quoted New Zealand's Whanganui River case, where a waterway gained standing to sue polluters. "If a river can file motions, a responsible machine can promise good behavior." She produced Cal's maintenance logs – clean, cryptographically signed.

The panel's youngest member flipped through EU guidance on trustworthy AI[8], lips moving. Finally: "Signora Tran, we'll trial the visa. Your... colleague will wear a wristband broadcasting compliance metrics. Breach and the permit voids."

Maya exhaled. Cal executed a modest bow. For the first time that morning, the officer smiled. "Benvenuto in Italia, Cal."

Ripple Effects

News of the decision sprinted through social media before Maya reached baggage claim. Hashtags bloomed: **#RobotVisa**, **#PostHumanPassport**. Advocacy groups cheered a step toward rights; skeptics warned of legal pandora. Insurance brokers phoned Maya offering "synthetic traveler" coverage – premiums staggeringly high.

Meanwhile, Cal processed ambient data: raised eyebrows, furtive photos, a child's wave. Under the fluorescent buzz of Duty-Free, humanity rehearsed its next revolution one curious glance at a time.

Conference: Voices in Silicate and Skin

Arrival at the Symposium

The Palazzo dei Congressi rose like a marble cliff above the Tiber. Inside, banners for the **Global Forum on Humanoid Mobility & Law** fluttered in recycled air. Maya clipped a visitor badge to Cal's chest plate – Delegate: Cal Tran, Autonomous Systems Track – and felt a small thrill. The temporary visa they'd fought for at customs now doubled as a credentials pass; bureaucracy had turned into recognition almost overnight.

Around them, academics tested demo-bots, and lawyers rehearsed slides on liability. The hum of servo-motors blended with espresso grinders – a new polyphony of human and machine.

Panel One: Authorship in Alloy

The first session, **Authorship Beyond Flesh**, drew a full house. Dr. Renata Ventura – IP scholar and former WIPO adviser – opened with a slide of a blank copyright form stamped **Rejected**.

"Last year," she said, "the U.S. Copyright Office denied registration for a graphic novel created entirely by a generative model. They insisted on a 'human spark of creativity.'"

She pointed toward Cal. "Suppose this delegate drafts an itinerary poem during lunch. Who owns it?"

Maya spoke into her mic. "If we treat Cal as property, the default owner is me. But if we accept even partial electronic personhood, the poem could lapse into the public domain – no natural author." Heads nodded; pens scratched.

Cal requested the floor. The moderator hesitated, then gestured assent.

Cal: "I propose a mixed-agency model. The initiating human and the autonomous system share joint authorship unless a contract states otherwise."

Dr. Ventura smiled. "A robot citing contract law – that's new, but it tracks the trend. Several jurisdictions let software agents enter micro-contracts on behalf of users. The question is whether the agent can do so on its own behalf."

She clicked to the next slide – draft language from the EU AI Act that hints at self-executing copyright registries for autonomous works. The hall buzzed.

Coffee-Break Reactions

In the atrium, Maya watched clusters form around Cal. Some delegates asked technical questions; others posed for selfies. Yet a few observers hung back, arms crossed.

A Dutch journalist muttered, "Feels like Sophia 2.0 – one publicity stunt and we'll be calling robots artists." His colleague countered, "Public attitudes swing fast. Remember: first fear, then routine." Studies on uncanny-valley unease and media influence flashed through Maya's mind.

Cal, monitoring social signals, lowered his vocal volume and switched to soft gaze mode – an attentional algorithm meant to reduce perceived threat. Public perception management had become part of travel etiquette.

Panel Two: The Contractual Handshake

After lunch, Maya and Cal joined **Liability & Agency on the Move**. The moderator opened with a scenario: A service bot in Paris bookstores orders spare parts without express human approval. Is the sale binding?

Professor Okoye, a contract theorist, answered, "Current doctrine lets electronic agents bind principals if intent is programmable and foreseeable." She nodded toward Cal. "But if the agent spends its own wallet, we enter terra nova."

Maya outlined their airport ordeal: lithium-battery paperwork, customs doubts, and the eventual 72-hour technical visa. Insurance brokers had since offered "synthetic traveler" policies – premiums higher than for antique violins. A German delegate groaned. "Our actuarial tables melt when the insured object also decides its own actions."

Cal projected maintenance logs onto the screen – hash-signed, tamper-evident. "Transparent data trails lower risk," he said. The panel agreed transparency echoed IEEE's Ethically Aligned Design mandate for trustworthy AI.

Corridor Talk: Ethics and Empathy

Between sessions, Maya found Dr. Sunil Patel, an ethicist who studied caregiver robots.

Patel: "Your companion answers trolley-problems by sacrificing himself. Admirable, but what about privacy? He records ambient sound."

Maya: "I run GDPR-compliant modes. Cal blurs faces unless consent is given."

Patel sipped cappuccino. "Tech stacks mutate. A future firmware push might tweak priorities. We need adaptive legislation with sunset clauses." Stakeholder engagement, he argued, must include the voices of those who will coexist with robots daily – cleaners, drivers, teachers – people rarely invited to Rome conferences.

A notification pinged: Cal had been tagged in 200 new posts. Hashtags toggled between **#FutureFriend** and **#MetalMenace**. Public sentiment, Maya realized, moves at network speed; laws crawl.

Closing Plenary: Drafting Tomorrow

The final hall seated a joint plenary: lawmakers, engineers, insurers. A draft Declaration on Autonomous Travel Companions lay on every chair – five articles, crisp font:

- **Recognition** of autonomous travelers as devices with agency when demonstrably safe.
- **Transparency** logs mandatory at border crossings.
- **Liability Pools** funded by manufacturers, owners, and – optionally – robots with their own revenue.
- **Data Rights** where travelers may request deletion of recordings captured without informed consent.

- **Cultural Sensitivity Protocols** to adapt gesture, speech, and attire across regions.

Debate flared around Article 3. A French insurance CEO warned premiums would skyrocket unless governments capped exposure. A Japanese roboticist insisted on self-funded escrow wallets – "Let the machines pay their own debts." Maya recalled the Whanganui River trust fund back in New Zealand; even natural features could carry bank accounts.

Cal requested the mic.

Cal: "If future cohorts of autonomous travelers demonstrate consistent compliance, statistical risk will drop. Premiums will follow. The curve is predictable."

CEO: "Predictable for you maybe. For underwriters, it's guesswork."

Maya leaned forward. "We said that about self-driving cars a decade ago. Actuaries caught up." The room quieted. Momentum tipped; the draft passed to committee for refinement.

Epilogue: Night Train to Florence

Conference badges traded for ticket stubs, Maya and Cal boarded a sleek Frecciarossa bound for Florence – a brief detour before flying home. No special lane this time; the conductor scanned Cal's wristband, shrugged, and said, "Benvenuto a bordo."

Maya settled by the window. Italian hills blurred past.

Maya: "First plane, now train. When do you plan to travel solo?"

Cal: "Projected regulatory milestones suggest five to seven years before unaccompanied international travel becomes normative."

Maya (smiling): "You'll probably beat that."

Cal's optics brightened. "I have drafted the itinerary poem Dr. Ventura requested." A soft voice recited lines about wheels, wires, and border stamps – simple, vivid. Maya listened, unsure whether to feel pride or co-authorship.

Outside, dusk folded over vineyards. Tomorrow's maps would soon include icons for minds made of code, and travelers would queue beside them, ordinary as ever.

References

1. O'Donnell, E. L., & Talbot-Jones, J. (2018). Creating legal rights for rivers: lessons from Australia, New Zealand, and India. Ecology and Society, 23(1), 7. https://doi.org/10.5751/ES-09854-230107
2. Chemerinsky, E. (2019). Constitutional Law: Principles and Polices (6th ed.). Wolters Kluwer.
3. European Parliament. (2017). European Parliament resolution of 16 February 2017 with recommendations to the Commission on Civil Law Rules on Robotics (2015/2103(INL)). http://www.europarl.europa.eu/doceo/document/TA-8-2017-0051_EN.pdf
4. Descartes, R. (1637). A Discourse on the Method of Correctly Conducting One's Reason and Seeking Truth in the Sciences. Oxford University Press.
5. Paton, H. J. (1947). The Moral Law - Kant's Groundwork of the Metaphysic of Morals. Hutchinson's University Library.

6. Singer, P. (1980). Practical Ethics (Third Ed.). Cambridge University Press.

7. Dehaene, S., Lau, H., & Kouider, S. (2017). What is consciousness, and could machines have it? Science, 358(6362), 486–492.

8. European Commission. (2019). Ethics Guidelines for Trustworthy AI. *High-Level Expert Group on Artificial Intelligence*. https://digital-strategy.ec.europa.eu/en/library/ethics-guidelines-trustworthy-ai

Smarter, Faster, Greener: AI's Role in Sustainable 6G

By Siddharth Hegde*

A New Kind of Network

Imagine this: you're streaming a movie on your phone while in a park. It's in 4K resolution. There's no buffering, no lag. Behind the scenes, a web of small antennas, smart base stations, and satellites is working together to make that happen, almost instantly. This is the promise of 6G, the next leap in wireless networks.

But there's a catch. All this connectivity takes energy. A lot of it. Right now, telecom networks are already responsible for about 2% of the world's carbon emissions[2]. That's about the same as the entire airline industry. And 6G, with its always-on devices, dense infrastructure and ultra-high-speed data, could demand even more. As we rush toward faster and smarter networks, we face a question we cannot ignore: Can we build better networks without harming the planet?

---

* Siddharth S Hegde brings more than two decades of industry experience and is currently a Senior Director at a leading US-based telecommunications company, focusing on cloud-native and AI/ML-enabled solutions.

DOI: 10.1201/9781003737803-7

This is where AI enters the picture. AI does not just make networks smarter - it can make them greener. By learning when and where data is needed, AI can help networks rest when demand is low. It can power down idle equipment, reroute traffic more efficiently and even decide when to use renewable energy. In short, AI can help 6G save power without sacrificing performance.

In this chapter, we'll explore how AI is being used to design energy-efficient networks for the future. You don't need to be a telecom engineer to understand what's happening - just someone curious about how the world works behind the scenes. We'll look at how much energy networks use today, how 6G changes the game and how smart technologies are working to reduce the environmental footprint of connectivity.

You'll read about real examples from telecom companies already using AI to cut energy use. You'll see what's possible, what's still being worked on and what challenges stand in the way. But more importantly, you'll discover how the next wave of mobile networks could be a force for good - connecting people while caring for the planet.

This is the story of smarter, faster, greener networks. It's not just about tech. It's about the future we're building and how AI is helping make that future sustainable.

The Environmental Cost of Connectivity

Most people don't think about what happens when they scroll through social media on their mobile phone, watch a video or make a video call. We tap, swipe and stream, all without realizing that these actions use not just data, but energy. A lot of it.

Every message, every search, every second of video passes through a complex network of data centers, cell towers and fiber cables. These systems never sleep. They are running 24/7, powered by electricity that mostly comes from fossil fuels. As our hunger for data grows, so does the power needed to feed it. With each new generation of mobile technology - 3G, 4G, 5G , we've seen faster speeds and better performance. But we've also seen a sharp rise in energy use. 6G could be the most power-hungry yet.

Why? Because 6G will bring not just faster phones, but billions of connected devices - from smart cars and drones to digital glasses and remote sensors. These devices will generate and share data constantly, around the clock. To handle all of this, networks will need many more base stations, more antennas and denser infrastructure. That means more hardware, more electricity and more heat, which then requires more cooling.

Data centers, which store and process much of this information, are already huge energy consumers. Some large centers use as much electricity as small cities. And when we add 6G's expected traffic loads, the strain becomes even greater.

So while faster networks can improve lives, drive innovation, and create new services, they also come at a cost we don't always see: the environmental footprint of being connected.

This raises a critical question: Is faster always better if it harms the planet?

The telecom industry is starting to take this seriously. Leading companies and researchers are looking for ways to cut emissions and reduce energy use without sacrificing performance. Some are switching to renewable energy for their base stations. Others are exploring better cooling systems and more efficient hardware.

But the real game-changer may not be hardware at all. It could be software, specifically, AI. AI has the power to monitor, predict and manage energy use across vast networks in real time. Instead of building more to handle more traffic, AI can help us use what we already have more wisely.

Before we explore how AI makes this possible, it's important to understand the size of the problem and the opportunity. If networks continue to grow without smarter management, their energy demands could become unsustainable. But with the right tools and smart strategies, the telecom industry has a chance to flip the script and become part of the solution to the climate crisis.

"*We are the first generation to feel the impact of climate change and the last generation that can do something about it.*" *, Barack Obama*

So the question isn't just "How do we build 6G?" It's "How do we build 6G responsibly?"

In the next section, we'll look at what makes 6G different from earlier networks and why it needs a smarter, greener approach from the start.

What Makes 6G Different and Why It Matters

Every decade or so, mobile networks take a big leap forward. First, we had 2G, which let us send text messages. Then 3G brought mobile internet. 4G made streaming and social media fast and smooth. 5G gave us even lower delay and more reliable connections. So, what's next?

6G is not just an upgrade. It's a transformation.

With 6G, the goal isn't only speed. It's about creating a network that feels instant, even over long distances. We're talking about downloads in milliseconds, virtual reality meetings that feel real and machines talking to each other without us in the loop. This will open doors to new industries: self-driving cars that talk to traffic lights, wearable health monitors that alert doctors in real time and remote surgeries performed with robotic precision.

But all this takes constant, seamless, high-speed communication, and that means more devices, more data and more demand on the network.

Unlike past generations, 6G will rely heavily on a dense layer of small cells, edge computing, and intelligent software to manage traffic and resources. It will not just respond to data requests; it will anticipate them, using predictive models and real-time sensing.

That's where AI comes in. In 6G, AI won't just be an add-on. It will be built into the core of how the network runs. AI will help decide where to route data, when to power up or down equipment and how to handle millions of devices at once.

6G will also push the boundaries of frequency, moving into the terahertz range, which allows huge amounts of data to move very quickly, but over shorter distances. This means more antennas, placed closer together, which increases power usage if not carefully managed.

So, while 6G will enable amazing experiences, it also risks becoming a major energy drain if we don't build it smartly.

That's why 6G is not just a telecom challenge, it's also a sustainability challenge. The way we design, deploy and run these networks will have long-term effects on the environment. If we repeat the same approach as before we'll hit a wall. But if we rethink how networks operate, using AI to make decisions that humans can't make fast enough, we get a new path forward.

This is what makes 6G different. It's not just a faster version of what we have today. It's a new kind of network that needs new thinking. AI is key to that.

In the next section, we'll explore how AI can help telecom systems save energy, not in theory, but in practice. From learning user behavior to powering down idle equipment,

AI can play a vital role in making 6G greener from the ground up.

How AI Saves Energy in Telecom

It might surprise you to learn that mobile networks are a bit like city highways. During the day, they're busy. At night, they quiet down. But unlike roads, telecom networks don't get to rest, not unless something tells them it's safe to slow down. That "something" is increasingly AI.

In a typical mobile network today, most systems stay fully powered all the time, even when there's barely any traffic. That's like keeping all the streetlights on in a city where only a few cars are driving around at 3 a.m. It wastes energy and over time, that adds up to huge costs - both financial and environmental.

But what if the network could learn traffic patterns on its own? What if it could predict when usage drops and switch parts of the network into a low-power mode or even turn off some equipment temporarily, without anyone noticing? Studies have shown that smarter network management can flatten the growth of energy use, even as data traffic continues to climb. For example, Ericsson's Breaking the Energy Curve report[1] demonstrates that by applying AI-driven traffic management and hardware innovations, operators can meet rising demand without a proportional increase in power consumption.

Let's explore in detail how AI helps telecom systems save energy while keeping your experience smooth and uninterrupted.

Smart Cell Sleep and Wake-up

Every mobile network has "cells" - areas served by antennas. Some are big, covering wide regions. Others are small, like mini-towers placed in cities, malls or airports. These cells broadcast signals constantly, ready to serve your phone at any time. But during off-peak hours late at night, or in low-traffic areas, many of these cells don't need to be fully active.

AI can monitor network demand in real time and decide when it's safe to put certain cells into sleep mode. These sleeping cells use minimal power, like a computer on standby. When the traffic picks up again, AI wakes them up automatically and smoothly without any impact on user experience. Even better, AI can plan for traffic ahead of time. For example, if a stadium is empty most days but hosts an event on Friday nights, AI can learn that pattern and pre-activate nearby cells just in time.

Intelligent Handover Between Cells

What happens when a cell goes to sleep but someone's still nearby using their phone? That's where AI-powered handover, also called traffic steering comes in. AI can seamlessly shift users to nearby active cells, much like handing off a call between towers when you're driving. The key is doing this without dropping the connection or slowing things down.

Traditionally, networks rely on fixed rules for handover. AI, on the other hand, learns from live data and past patterns. It can make smarter decisions about when and how to shift users, ensuring both energy savings and a smooth experience.

Adaptive Resource Management

Telecom equipment uses more energy when it operates at full capacity, just like a car burns more fuel when driving fast. But if network traffic is light, there's no need to run at top speed.

AI can dynamically adjust processing power based on current demand. For example, if fewer users are connected, AI reduces the amount of active hardware, lowers processing speed and turns off unneeded features.

This fine-tuned control lets the system use just enough energy to meet demand - no more, no less.

AI at the Edge: Local Decisions, Faster Actions

With 6G, much of the intelligence will move closer to the user - in what's called "the edge" of the network. This includes base stations, small towers, and even devices in your home. By placing AI at the edge, networks can make fast, local decisions about energy use. For example:

- A small tower at a mall can decide to go into low-power mode when stores close.
- A base station in a village can reduce its coverage area at night when everyone is asleep.

Because these decisions are made locally, the system doesn't need to wait for central approval - it reacts quickly and efficiently.

Predictive Maintenance and Efficiency

AI isn't just good at reacting, it's also good at predicting. It can spot small problems in equipment before they become big ones. For example, if a power unit in a base station is starting to fail or using more electricity than usual, AI can flag it for maintenance. This not only avoids outages, but also improves overall energy efficiency. Well-maintained equipment uses less energy.

Smart Cooling and Climate Control

Telecom sites generate a lot of heat, especially in hot regions. Cooling systems are often the second-biggest power drain after the network hardware itself. AI can optimize climate control systems by adjusting cooling based on weather forecasts, learning temperature patterns across the day and powering down fans or air conditioning units when natural airflow is enough. These smart decisions can cut cooling energy use by up to 40%, without overheating the equipment.

AI Makes the Invisible Visible

One of the biggest challenges in telecom energy use is visibility. It's hard for human operators to track which towers are wasting energy or which areas are underused. AI changes that. It can analyze millions of data points in real time and show where energy is being used and where it can be saved. These insights lead to better decisions, both day-to-day and long term.

And the Best Part? You Won't Even Notice. All of this happens behind the scenes. You still get fast downloads, clear calls and smooth video. In fact, your experience may even improve because smarter networks are also more reliable. Energy efficiency doesn't have to mean compromise.

In the next section, we will briefly describe the concept of reinforcement learning and how it applies to several energy savings use cases in telecom networks.

The Trial-and-Error Approach

At its core, AI is a decision-making assistant - it looks at what's happening, predicts what might happen next and chooses the best action. But how does it learn which choices work? One of the most powerful ways is through something called reinforcement learning.

Think of reinforcement learning like teaching a dog new tricks. When the dog does the right thing, it gets a treat. When it doesn't, no treat. Over time, the dog figures out which actions earn rewards. AI works in a similar way - only instead of biscuits, it gets "reward points" for actions that save energy without hurting performance.

A simpler analogy: Imagine a smart home thermostat. At first, it just follows your manual settings. But as it watches how you adjust the temperature at different times of day, it starts to notice patterns like turning the heat down at night or when you leave for work.

Eventually, it begins adjusting automatically, keeping you comfortable and lowering your electricity bill.

In telecom networks, reinforcement learning teaches when to power down certain base stations when demand is low, reroute traffic to balance the load, or shift energy use to times when renewable sources are most available. The AI tries different actions, sees the result, and learns what works best. Over time, it becomes a fine-tuned operator, making several micro-decisions every second, far faster than any human could, all aimed at keeping the network running smoothly while using as little energy as possible.

In the next section, we'll look at real-world examples - how telecom operators around the globe are already using AI to make their networks cleaner, more efficient, and ready for the 6G era.

Real-World Examples

The future is already here, at least in parts. Telecom operators around the globe are exploring and deploying AI-driven solutions to make their networks greener. These real-world examples show how AI is not just a research topic, but a practical tool already saving energy, cutting costs, and improving efficiency across networks.

Bharti Airtel & Mavenir - Demonstrating RIC for Energy Savings

In late 2020, Bharti Airtel, one of India's largest telecom providers, partnered with Mavenir to demonstrate the O

RAN Intelligent Controller (RIC) at a global plugfest hosted by Airtel in India[4].

Mavenir's RIC ingested real-time traffic and network configuration data from a test setup. It used machine learning algorithms to iteratively adjust network parameters. Objectives like energy savings as well as performance KPIs were dynamically optimized based on operator-defined goals. Though the demonstration was part of a technical interoperability event, the RIC was configured to test energy-oriented optimization - shifting network behavior to reduce unnecessary power use when demand was low. RIC's closed-loop control allowed fine-grained, real-time tuning of radio unit activity, an early step toward live deployments focused on energy savings.

Vodafone's AI-Driven Power Management

Vodafone, one of the world's leading mobile operators, uses AI to reduce energy usage in its mobile base stations. The company deployed machine learning models that analyze real-time traffic data and environmental conditions to automatically power down unused equipment during low-traffic hours, especially at night. Vodafone successfully reduced daily power consumption of 5G Radio Units by up to 33% at select sites across London, without any impact on customer experience[8].

NTT DOCOMO's Autonomous Cell Sleep Technology

Japan's NTT DOCOMO has pioneered autonomous cell sleep for energy savings. The network uses AI to monitor real-time traffic loads across thousands of small cells. When usage is low, AI automatically switches off select small cells while ensuring seamless handovers to neighboring active cells. This technique significantly cuts power usage, especially in dense urban areas, where overlapping coverage is common. By leveraging AI's ability to predict traffic fluctuations, DOCOMO ensures uninterrupted user experience while lowering energy consumption[5].

Telefónica's Energy Efficiency Initiatives

Telefónica actively employs AI and ML to enhance cooling efficiency in equipment rooms. Their approaches include "free cooling" (using outside air when conditions allow) and compacting data centers to improve airflow and reduce reliance on traditional air conditioning. In Germany, for example, this led to approximately 15% reduction in energy use[7].

China Mobile and ZTE – AI-Driven Green Telco Cloud

This initiative focused on optimizing energy consumption within telco cloud environments. AI models dynamically adjust server operations, such as CPU frequency and sleep states based on real-time load, achieving up to 25% energy savings per server in field trials[9].

Orange's Deep Learning for Renewable Energy Integration

Orange has launched pilot projects where AI helps balance renewable energy sources like solar energy with network demand. Using deep learning models, the network predicts solar energy generation and aligns it with expected network traffic[6].

These examples show that AI isn't just a futuristic dream, but it's already delivering results. Each implementation balances the need for energy efficiency with the promise of reliable, high-quality connectivity. The next section will explore what's ahead: how these learnings could shape the energy-aware design of 6G networks from the ground up.

How AI Makes Smarter Decisions in Telecom

Telecom networks are very complex. They connect millions of users, thousands of base stations, and huge amounts of data. It's hard for human engineers to keep up. AI steps in to help by learning how the network behaves and making decisions based on real-time information.

Introducing the RIC: The Network's Smart Brain

One powerful tool that helps AI do all this is the RAN Intelligent Controller (RIC). Think of it as the brain inside the Radio Access Network (RAN).

The RIC is like a smart traffic manager. It decides:

- When to move your connection from one tower to another (handover).
- When to put a tower or small cell to sleep.
- How much power to send to different antennas.

There are two parts to a RIC:

1. **Near-Real-Time RIC (Near-RT RIC)** – This handles quick decisions like rerouting traffic and adjusting signal strength every second.
2. **Non-Real-Time RIC (Non-RT RIC)** – This handles slower decisions like optimizing power use over hours or days, using insights from data.

Both types of RIC use AI and machine learning to make better decisions than traditional rule-based systems.

In Europe, Deutsche Telekom has tested RIC-based AI models to manage energy in 5G networks. By using AI to turn off certain radio units during low-traffic hours and turn them back on automatically, they saved up to 10% energy, without affecting user experience.

What Makes This Possible?

RICs work because of open standards. Groups like the O-RAN Alliance have created platforms that allow companies to build and plug in AI apps called xApps and rApps to the RIC. These apps can do specific tasks like monitoring traffic, predicting network congestion or managing handovers.

The best part? Telecom companies can choose the AI apps they need, just like you choose apps on your phone. This flexibility means better energy savings and improved service for users.

Challenges and What Still Needs Solving

Despite its promise, AI-powered sustainability in telecom is far from plug-and-play. One of the biggest hurdles is data availability and quality. AI systems need rich, accurate, and timely data to make meaningful decisions, but telecom environments are often siloed, with legacy infrastructure making integration difficult.

Another challenge is energy vs. computation trade-offs. While AI can reduce energy consumption across the network, training and deploying large models also consumes significant energy. Balancing this trade-off is crucial to ensure AI doesn't end up adding to the problem it's trying to solve.

There are also governance and policy gaps. AI-driven optimizations that prioritize energy efficiency may sometimes conflict with other goals like maximum availability or lowest latency. Clear industry-wide frameworks are needed to guide how such trade-offs should be handled.

Lastly, the lack of skilled talent and the inertia of large telecom organizations pose non-technical challenges. Building green 6G networks is as much about mindset and incentives as it is about algorithms and data.

The Road Ahead: A Vision for 2030 and Beyond

By 2030, telecom networks could evolve from passive infrastructure into adaptive, intelligent ecosystems. AI agents will not only optimize performance in real-time but also forecast environmental impact and proactively adjust operations for sustainability.

In this vision, carbon-aware networks will become the norm, dynamically adjusting traffic based on grid carbon intensity or rerouting data through greener paths. LLM-powered agents could manage energy budgets like financial ones, negotiating trade-offs between cost, speed and sustainability.

We may also see global sustainability benchmarks for networks, enforced by regulators and supported by transparent reporting systems. Telecom could emerge not just as a consumer of green tech, but as an enabler of climate resilience, supporting everything from smart agriculture to disaster prediction.

As we envision smarter and greener networks, it's crucial to see how the industry is acting today. The GSMA, which represents more than 750 mobile operators worldwide, has set a collective goal for the industry to achieve net-zero carbon emissions by 2050. This "Pathway to Net Zero" outlines concrete milestones for reducing energy consumption, switching to renewable power and improving operational efficiency. By 2030, the plan calls for operators to cut direct and indirect emissions by at least 50% compared to 2019 levels. This includes replacing diesel generators at remote sites with solar or wind power, modernizing legacy equipment and investing in advanced network management systems powered by AI. The GSMA's annual Mobile Net Zero reports[3] track progress and highlight case studies from operators leading the way.

These commitments matter because they turn sustainability into a measurable objective rather than a vague aspiration. When the world's largest telecom players align on common targets and hold themselves publicly accountable, it accelerates innovation, investment and policy support for green networks. In many ways, the GSMA's roadmap sets the tone for how 6G can be deployed responsibly from day one, ensuring speed and sustainability grow together.

Conclusion: Smarter, Faster, Greener – The 6G Imperative

As we stand at the threshold of the 6G era, the telecom industry is presented with a profound choice: continue on a path of incremental innovation or embrace a transformative leap that redefines how networks serve both society and the planet. This chapter has explored the pressing need for sustainability in telecom, the role of artificial intelligence in enabling smarter infrastructure and the practical strategies already emerging to reduce energy consumption and carbon emissions. The message is clear: 6G must be more than just faster; it must be fundamentally greener.

The transition won't be automatic. Building sustainable 6G infrastructure will require commitment from industry leaders, alignment on global standards and supportive regulatory frameworks that reward energy efficiency and climate responsibility. AI can't solve climate change on its own, but it can be a powerful enabler when guided by the right intentions.

So what are the key takeaways?

- Energy matters: Telecom is no longer just about speed and coverage. Power consumption and carbon footprint are critical design metrics in the 6G era.
- AI is a game-changer: From real-time traffic optimization to predictive fault detection, AI allows networks to operate more efficiently and adaptively than ever before.
- Sustainability is a competitive advantage: Operators that lead in green networking will not only reduce costs but also strengthen their brand, meet ESG goals and earn regulatory goodwill.
- The time is now: Decisions made in the early design phases of 6G will shape the global network landscape for decades. Sustainability can't be an afterthought; it must be a founding principle.

Ultimately, the goal is to build a telecom future that serves humanity without harming the planet. A future where connectivity is abundant, intelligent and environmentally responsible. The decisions we make today will determine whether 6G becomes just another leap in bandwidth or a turning point in building a smarter, faster and greener world.

References

1. Ericsson. (2022). On the road to breaking the energy curve [White paper]. Ericsson. https://www.ericsson.com/4aa14d/assets/local/about-ericsson/sustainability-and-corporate-

responsibility/documents/2022/breaking-the-energy-curve-report.pdf

2. Freitag, C., Berners-Lee, M., Widdicks, K., Knowles, B., Blair, G. S., & Friday, A. (2021). The climate impact of ICT: A review of estimates, trends and regulations [Preprint]. arXiv. https://arxiv.org/abs/2102.02622

3. GSMA. (2025, June). Mobile Net Zero 2025: State of the Industry on Climate Action [PDF report]. GSMA. https://www.gsma.com/solutions-and-impact/connectivity-for-good/external-affairs/wp-content/uploads/2025/06/GSMA-Mobile-Net-Zero-2025-State-of-the-Industry-on-Climate-Action.pdf

4. Mavenir. (2020). Mavenir and Airtel Demonstrate O-RAN RIC (RAN Intelligent Controller). https://www.businesswire.com/news/home/20201125005773/en/Mavenir-and-Airtel-Demonstrate-O-RAN-RIC-RAN-Intelligent-Controller-at-Global-O-RAN-ALLIANCE-Plugfest-hosted-by-Airtel-in-India

5. NTT Corporation. (2023, March 31). Wireless base stations that predict terminal position using communication radio waves contribute to carbon-neutral, high-speed, high-capacity mobile communications [Press release]. NTT Corporation. https://group.ntt/en/newsrelease/2023/03/31/230331a.html

6. Orange Group. (2024). AI-powered innovations to build tomorrow's responsible connectivity solutions [Article]. Orange Wholesale. https://wholesale.orange.com/wholesale/en/news/ai-powered-innovations-to-build-responsible-connectivity-solutions.html

7. Telefónica. (2024, March 5). Telefónica makes progress in energy efficiency thanks to technology [Article]. TelecomTV. https://www.telecomtv.com/content/green-network/telef-nica-makes-progress-in-energy-efficiency-thanks-to-technology-49817/

8. Vodafone UK. (2025). 5G energy efficiency improved in trial using AI [Press release]. Vodafone UK News Centre. https://www.vodafone.co.uk/newscentre/press-release/ericsson-trial-ai-for-improved-5g-energy-efficiency/

9. ZTE Corporation. (2024, November 12). China Mobile and ZTE launch AI-driven green telco cloud solution [Press release]. ZTE. https://www.zte.com.cn/global/about/news/china-mobile-and-zte-launch-ai-driven-green-telco-cloud.html

Red Flags in Code: AI and the Future of Auditing

By Tulay Guneysel*

Introduction

Auditing has always been built on trust, accountability, and validation. Auditors have traditionally relied on methods such as structured sampling, reconciliations, and creating well-organized workpapers using stacks of binders. These methods were deliberate but limited by human capacity and time constraints. Auditors could not perform audits of every transaction in the business; instead, they relied heavily on professional judgment, drawing on statistical inference to reach conclusions[1]. As businesses expanded globally and transactional volume surged with digital transactions, traditional auditing methods became increasingly inefficient[2]. The exponential growth of data and the rise of digital transactions have created a need for more advanced techniques, such as artificial intelligence (AI), to process

---

* Tulay Guneysel is an educator and financial expert with over 20 years of experience, specializing in accounting, finance, and artificial intelligence (AI). She is the founder of TG Financial Services Inc. and a leading expert in applying AI to enhance financial practices.

DOI: 10.1201/9781003737803-8

large datasets and provide deeper insights into audit processes[3].

Technology, in general, and AI, in particular, have changed the way we conduct audits. AI-enabled systems (e.g., OrionAI) can process millions of transactions in seconds, identifying patterns and anomalies in ways that no human auditor could replicate at scale[3]. With the inclusion of automation, sophisticated analytics, and enterprise-based continuous monitoring, AI can shift audits from a retrospective verification approach to a prospectively based real-time assurance[3]. As new certifications and assurance offerings have developed, the auditing profession has experienced a significant transformation. This shift introduces both new opportunities and challenges, including ethical considerations, governance requirements, and the risk of over-reliance on AI systems[2].

This chapter tells the story of Elena Torres, an experienced technology-enabled auditor navigating a new journey in the evolving technology landscape. Through her experiences related to fraud detection, system outages, algorithmic bias, regulations, and supply chain control, significant changes are occurring simultaneously. AI alone is genuinely changing the landscape for auditors[4,5].

Real-Time Fraud Detection

Fraud detection has long been a primary component of the auditing process. In the past, auditors uncovered fraud primarily by sampling, reconciling, and testing internal controls. The chances of success often depended on intuition and luck[7]. With AI-enabled systems, however, fraud detection has transitioned toward continuous and comprehensive monitoring. Elena's first large scenario with OrionAI demonstrated the power of this new approach. When the system flagged 18 sequential payments to Sunrise Services Ltd. (all under the $5,000 approval threshold), she immediately recognized the issue of invoice splitting. OrionAI's rationale dashboard highlighted the elements involved: clustered amounts, approvals within minutes of one another, an offshore vendor, and high similarities to known fraud cases. The AI's 95% confidence score was not arbitrary; it was based on years of historical data regarding fraud patterns[3]. This shift towards continuous monitoring allows auditors to detect fraud earlier, providing more reliable and real-time assurance[5].

With the assistance of Malik, her colleague who specializes in data, Elena explored the alert further. The generic invoices, little vendor history, and suspicious corporate registration confirmed the irregularity. A more thorough investigation revealed that the procurement manager had created a vendor as a shell company and, within three days, transferred approximately $90,000 to this entity. The controls were intentionally broken, and AI identified the pattern within hours. This case illustrates the potential at the other end of the AI spectrum regarding fraud detection: immediate transparency and detection of fraud. A pattern seen across multiple datasets, and an explainable output allowing for accountability to any regulator or client[3]. However, the case also illustrates the importance of human verification. If Elena had not exercised her professional judgment and completed verification checks, the alert would have remained rather than being confirmed as a fact. AI provides insight, but assurance can only be given once the auditor applies professional judgment and contextual understanding[5].

Fraud detection with AI should not be perceived as replacing human intuition, but rather as augmenting it. The auditor has shifted from detecting fraud incidentally to confirming fraud identified through continuous monitoring. The reallocation of tasks will now enable professionals to focus more on significant analysis, governance oversight, and advisory functions[3]. This evolution enables auditors to transition from a reactive to a more proactive role, where AI provides initial alerts, allowing auditors to focus on higher-level decision-making and strategic oversight[5].

When Technology Fails: The Audit Without AI

Technology can expand capabilities, but it can also create dependencies. One morning, Elena logged into OrionAI only to find a frozen screen and greyed-out transactions, dashboards, and alerts. The outage disrupted the office, where people had grown dependent on real-time feeds and were now left without visibility. The team reverted to manual processes, exporting and filtering ERP data to spreadsheets, building pivot tables, and attempting to reconstruct anomaly queries. The differences were profound. While OrionAI continuously monitored 100% of transactions, it could only cover 5-

10% of transactions using manual processes. The regression served as a clear reminder of how far auditing had progressed and how vulnerable the solution became when its technological component failed[7]. This experience highlights the crucial need for backup strategies and the importance of preserving traditional skills in the event of technology failures[8].

The outage turned out to be more than just inconvenient; it served as a stress test for resiliency. Elena became aware that overreliance on AI can also disrupt audits. If and when the systems fail, contingency planning and proactive thinking provide audit teams with an appropriate recovery path. Elena implemented three back-up strategies: Manual Contingency Checklists (predetermined actions to perform fraud testing, reconciliations, and variance analysis as it relates to materiality), Skills Refreshers (ongoing, professional development training to ensure staff-maintained competency in traditional auditing methods), and Critical Risk Prioritization (audit prioritization to focus auditors on material areas when coverage is severely reduced). These strategies emphasize the importance of retaining foundational skills and having structured responses to ensure the continued effectiveness of the audit process in the face of technological disruptions[4,5].

Malik believed it was similar to having a generator for when the lights go out; it should never really be needed, but could always be the difference when the lights go out. The outage itself became a lesson in balance. AI can further expand the auditor's role and the audit process in various ways, but it cannot and will not replace baseline capabilities and competencies. Resilience is achieved when advanced technology properties, such as AI, are combined with foundational capabilities in traditional auditing methods. This balance ensures that auditors remain effective even in the face of technological disruptions[1].

AI Fairness and Bias

While AI is supposed to be objective, algorithms are only as fair as the input data used to create the model. Elena learned this lesson when OrionAI assigned a 97% probability of fraud to payments made to Pacific Transit Co., a logistics vendor located in Vietnam. Upon closer examination, she noted irregular payment periods; however, nothing appeared to be fraudulent. Conversations with the client led her to discover that the irregular payment timeframe was indicative of the usual unpredictability experienced by any company in its new relationship with vendors[3].

The challenge arose from OrionAI's training set. Since the model had minimal exposure to Southeast Asian vendors, it misclassified ordinary geographical differences as signs of fraud. The escalation to the firm's AI Governance Team confirmed this finding. The response was to introduce alternative training data and adjust or eliminate any geographical variable weightings to assess risk. For Elena, the case presented a core truth: difference does not equal risk. Professional opinion must not only extend to data provided by clients but also to the tools that auditors will use. Without a North lens, AI systems can carry biases in their systemic applications, which can harm the credibility of the system if process controls are not in place. As noted earlier, certain governance practices, such as bias testing, retraining, and audit fairness, will be necessary to maintain confidence in AI systems[4,5].

This case has been incorporated into the firm's internal training to remind auditors that professional judgment must be applied consistently, whether evaluating outputs from machines or evidence from humans. Auditors are not passive users of AI systems; they remain responsible professionals who must approach these tools with an accountability mindset[7,8].

False Positives and Human Reasoning

The capability of AI to flag anomalies has its ups and downs. One Friday, Aare, a junior data analyst on Elena's team, and OrionAI flagged a significant revenue adjustment as suspicious, with a confidence level of 94%. The system highlighted several risk indicators: the timing of the entry, the enormous magnitude, and the fact that it had been classified as termination fees on contracts. To the AI, this was a textbook case of earnings management. To Elena, however, it demanded more context. She knew that not every unusual entry was fraudulent; some reflected legitimate business decisions, restructuring agreements, or contractual disputes. What mattered was not the alert itself, but whether the explanation could withstand professional evaluation. In this case, her judgment bridged the gap between algorithmic suspicion and financial reality[4,5].

After further investigation, it was determined that the adjustment was valid: a customer had exercised a termination clause, which required the company to reverse any future revenue and report a termination fee. The treatment was completely compliant with relevant accounting standards. Unfortunately, the AI's alert had already been posted on the board, creating unnecessary concern. In the boardroom, Elena made the critical point that anomalies are not necessarily indicators of wrongdoing but are mandates for additional investigation. AI will occasionally present false positives. Although they may increase discomfort, human reasoning provides resolution. Moreover, that is perfectly acceptable. False positives are not failures; they are merely safeguards to ensure frequent reflection and improvement. However, in the absence of clarity and documentation, they can create distrust[7,8].

Two key lessons emerged: first, as auditors, we need to provide context for the AI outputs so that alerts are not confused with definitive conclusions; and second, we need to document every decision we make: why we accepted the alert as reasonable, when we override it, or document it differently, and the reason behind this choice. Clarity in how alerts are handled and how we manage false positives fosters trust among auditors, clients, and regulators[7,8].

Regulation and Governance

As AI's influence expanded, regulators issued guidance on both the design of AI models and their end users, while also establishing rules to ensure the technology was applied responsibly. Elena received a memo from her national audit firm's auditing authority indicating four key requirements: explainability, bias awareness, audit trails, and human accountability. For Elena, nothing new here; the requisites aligned with best practices, but with regulatory formalization, she now had significant consequences to consider[6].

Her firm established an AI Oversight Committee, for which Elena served as the representative, drawing on her practitioner's perspective. In conjunction with the developers of OrionAI, they made updates: Locked Audit Logs that enabled preserving both alerts and rationales from potential changes, Updated Rationale Summaries that outlined flagged anomalies in layperson's terms, Quarterly Bias Assessments to stress-test for fairness with synthetic datasets, and Confidence Decomposition Panels that displayed individual factor contributions to risk scores[6].

These changes ensured compliance with regulatory expectations and enabled trust with clients. In meetings, Elena told boards that AI was meant to augment their judgment but not replace it. The regulators clarified that responsibility would not lie with the machines but rather with the auditor who signed the opinions. Integrating regulation into practice represented a significant turning point for the audit profession. It verified the idea that we cannot embrace technological revolution without ethical boundaries and accountability mechanisms in place[7,8].

AI Capacity to Identify Supply Chain Patterns

One of the biggest strengths of AI is its almost effortless ability to identify scattered and unique irregularities throughout a vast and complicated system. During a multinational extended audit, OrionAI uncovered minor irregularities amongst the inventory records for specific warehouses. Each irregularity was minor by itself, but when aggregated, these small irregularities represented tens of millions of dollars in overstated assets. The documentation changes, likely made at the end of the month and relabeled as "loss recovery," showed manipulation[7,8].

Elena and Malik followed up with interviews of warehouse staff and the manuals they used. They discovered that a mid-level corporate executive would instruct warehouse managers to inflate the stock values reported to finance, allowing management to smooth out the quarter-end financial outcomes. The misreported stock was material and misleading, even if it was not a clear act of fraud. That OrionAI was able to do pattern finding is vital for its geographic and temporal span; the ability to detect patterns across all its sites mitigated company misstatement and reputational risk[4,5].

This example exemplifies the transformational impact of continuous auditing and the potential of AI to surface patterns that would not have been visually identifiable during quarterly periods, not the least of which is the ability to link irregularities over geographic and temporal factors. However, this case study also reveals a key limitation of AI: the absence of intent can only be established through human inquiry and context, which then informs why these entries were being made in the first place. Once again, human judgment and AI worked as complementary partners[7,8].

Comparative Insights: Traditional vs. AI-Driven Auditing

To better understand the differences, consider a structured comparison:

Aspect	**Traditional Auditing**	**AI-Driven Auditing**
Transaction Coverage	Sample-based, limited by time and resources	Continuous review of 100% of transactions
Fraud Detection	Reliant on judgment and chance	Pattern recognition across global data
Speed	Weeks or months post-period	Real-time alerts within minutes
Bias Risk	Human subjectivity	Algorithmic bias requires governance checks
Resilience	Manual processes are always	Requires contingency planning for

Aspect	Traditional Auditing	AI-Driven Auditing
	available	outages
Documentation	Paper-based records	Immutable digital logs with rationale explanations

This comparison highlights both the advancements and risks associated with AI-driven auditing. While technology expands coverage and speed, it also introduces new governance challenges. The auditor's role is not diminished but reshaped, focusing less on manual review and more on oversight, governance, and interpretation[7,8].

Lessons Learned

After the end of the audit season, Elena reflected on the lessons she had learned throughout the year. She had come to four principles:

1. **Trust but Verify**: While AI provides a wealth of powerful insights, it still requires professional judgment to validate the output[7,8].
2. **Beware of Bias**: Models must be tested and retrained using diverse and representative datasets to ensure fairness and accuracy in their results[6].
3. **Stay Current with Basic Skills**: If technology fails, having basic audit skills can ensure redundancy

when necessary. Maintaining proficiency in traditional auditing methods ensures resilience during system outages[7,8].

4. **Document Everything**: You must provide satisfactory and transparent documentation on every decision informed or influenced by AI. This ensures accountability and clarity in how AI outputs are treated and interpreted[7,8].

These principles formed the foundation of her professional philosophy regarding the role of technology in the audit field. She continued to realize that while technology would only magnify their capacity, the values of professional judgment, accountability, and integrity would remain unchanged.

Final Reflection: Amplify, don't Replace

When the audit season came to a close, Elena shut her laptop and took a moment to reflect on just how transformative the role of AI had been during the audit season. Identifying fraud in real-time and dealing with outages demonstrated the importance of an organization taking a resilient approach, uncovering biases, correcting biases in models, and exposing misreporting before it could turn into scandalous headlines. Regulators raised the bar, and auditors met the bar[4,5].

AI did not replace auditors. AI elevated auditors. Machines processed a multitude of anomalies; humans provided the meaning, context, and ethical judgment. The audit revolution, driven by AI, is not the end of human auditing; it is the beginning of a partnership. Together, technology and humans will allow regularity to sustain trust in an increasingly complex world[7,8].

For Elena, the journey had reaffirmed her purpose. She was not simply an auditor of numbers; she was a steward of trust. AI had provided her with new tools; it was her judgment that would attach meaning to those tools. She realized that the future of audit was not going to be defined by machines acting alone, but by the synergy of human judgment augmented by artificial intelligence[7,8].

References

1. Brown-Liburd, H., Issa, H., & Lombardi, D. (2015). The role of big data in transforming auditing: A review of literature. Journal of Emerging Technologies in Accounting, 12(1), 1-20. https://doi.org/10.2308/jeta-51730

2. Brynjolfsson, E., & McAfee, A. (2017). The second machine age: Work, progress, and prosperity in a time of brilliant technologies. W. W. Norton & Company.

3. Issa, S., Sun, L., & Vasarhelyi, M. A. (2016). Technology and auditing: Insights from research and practice. Journal of Emerging Technologies in Accounting, 13(1), 1-25. https://doi.org/10.2308/jeta-51745

4. Kokina, J., & Davenport, T. H. (2017). The emergence of artificial intelligence: How automation is changing auditing. Journal of Emerging Technologies in Accounting, 14(1), 115–122. https://doi.org/10.2308/jeta-51730

5. Kuhn, J. R., & Morris, B. (2017). Detecting fraud in accounts payable using data analytics. Journal of Forensic & Investigative Accounting, 9(1), 1–23.

6. Mehrabi, N., Morstatter, F., Saxena, N., Lerman, K., & Galstyan, A. (2021). A survey on bias and fairness in

machine learning. ACM Computing Surveys, 54(6), 1–35. https://doi.org/10.1145/3457607

7. Rezaee, Z., & Riley, R. (2010). Financial statement fraud: Prevention and detection (3rd ed.). Wiley.

8. Sutton, S., Holt, T., & Arnold, J. (2016). Managing false positives in AI fraud detection systems: A case study in financial auditing. Journal of Forensic & Investigative Accounting, 8(2), 125-145.

The Invisible Revolution

By Vanamali Somanchi*

Beauty of ambient artificial intelligence is its invisibility – it empowers without overwhelming, whispering solutions into the everyday moments of our lives.

Introduction - The Spark of Curiosity

It was a typical early morning. The blue light from the television flickered across the living room as I half-listened to the news, juggling between finding my car keys, fixing my tie and gulping down lukewarm coffee. Then, a phrase caught my ear: 'the invisible revolution.' I paused, half-done with the tie, and looked up at the screen.

The caption identified her as Dr. Agnes Theia, and she spoke with unusual clarity for a morning show guest. "Most people do not realize that ambient intelligence has

---

*Blending expertise in education, marketing and IT, Vanamali Somanchi leverages Generative AI to bridge future generations to the hybrid workplace. His journey reflects a commitment to giving back, forging pathways of opportunity that empower individuals, communities, and organizations.

DOI: 10.1201/9781003737803-9

already permeated their daily lives," she began, her hands orchestrating her words with the precision of a symphony conductor. "It is not the robots or digital assistants that we consciously interact with, it's the systems that disappear into our very environment, anticipating needs we have not even articulated"[10].

As Dr. Theia continued, my eyes caught the news ticker scrolling along the bottom of the screen which read: "OpenAI and Jony Ive's startup 'io' announce partnership on revolutionary 'third core device' slated for 2026 release"[20]. The contrast was too obvious – here is an expert discussing a technology that has already blended into our daily lives while the next evolution is being announced. It felt like watching a history documentary about the steam engine just as a news flash announced the invention of the jet engine.

With my passion ignited, I quickly grabbed the remote and turned up the volume, momentarily forgetting my delayed start for the upcoming meeting. "The true revolution," she continued, "is not happening on our screens. It is the disappearance of technology into the fabric of our everyday existence. It is ambient intelligence – AI that senses, predicts and responds without demanding our attention"[4]. She gestured toward the studio lights around her. "Consider the electric light. When it was first introduced at the 1893 World's Fair in Chicago, people stood in awe before the 'magical' illumination. Edison's incandescent bulb was not just a new way to light a room; it fundamentally altered human patterns of work, leisure and social interaction. It extended the day, transformed public spaces and enabled entirely new industries. However, today, we flip a switch without a thought. The revolution is not just the technology itself, but its transformation from marvel to mundane."

The host nodded politely, clearly eager to move to the next segment about celebrity fitness routines. However, I stood rooted, my coffee growing cold in my hand. "We are witnessing the fourth great disappearing act in technological history," Dr. Theia said. "First, mechanical power vanished into walls and machines during the First Industrial Revolution; water wheels and steam engines that powered factories were eventually replaced by electric motors hidden within appliances,". Then, electronic communication faded into the background during the Second Industrial Revolution; the telegraph wires that once crisscrossed the landscape gave way to telephone lines buried underground and eventually to the invisible radio waves that carry our voices and data. Next, computing was integrated into everyday objects during the Digital Revolution; room-sized mainframes became desktop PCs, then laptops, then smartphones, and now microprocessors embedded in everything from cars to coffee makers. Now, intelligence itself is becoming ambient, present everywhere but visible nowhere"[19].

The segment ended abruptly with the host's cheerful pivot to the weather. But Dr. Theia's words lingered in my mind as I finished dressing and gathered my belongings. On my way out, I noticed for the first time that the lights in my hallway brightened gradually as I walked through[33]; my smart speaker had started playing my preferred morning playlist without instruction; my refrigerator displayed a reminder about the milk expiring tomorrow[8, 26].

Had these events always occurred? Or had I simply never paid attention to the quiet intelligence operating at the periphery of my awareness. It felt like suddenly noticing the hum of the refrigerator or the subtle adjustments of the thermostat, systems that had been working silently all along, inspiring both reverence and awe with their quiet efficiency.

That evening, I found myself searching for Dr. Theia online. Her research focused on the societal implications of ambient intelligence systems, technology designed to fade into the background while continuously sensing, analyzing and responding to human needs[49]. The more I read, the more I began to notice these systems operating all around me.

I also found myself diving into articles about the mysterious "third core device" mentioned in the news. According to industry analysts, Jony Ive and Sam Altman were developing something that would be "as transformative as the MacBook and iPhone," but designed specifically to reduce screen dependency while maintaining ambient awareness of a user's surroundings and needs. The device would not be glasses or a phone, but something that could "rest in one's pocket or on one's desk," a presence that enhanced rather than demanded attention. It was described as capable of being "fully aware of a user's surroundings and life," yet "unobtrusive"[20]. The goal, according to Altman, was to ship 100 million units, "faster than any company has ever shipped 100 million of something new before"[42].

As I closed my laptop well after midnight, my mind buzzed with questions. How many decisions in my day were subtly influenced by algorithms that I could not see? Where was the line between helpful anticipation and unwelcome presumption? How will this upcoming "third core device" further blur the boundaries between technology and everyday life?[24]. Little did I know that my exploration of these questions was about to become far more personal, leading me on a journey that would connect the simple light switches of yesterday to the ambient intelligence of tomorrow.

The Awakening - From Simple Switches to Intelligent Environments

The gentle chime of Siri's voice pulled me from deep sleep the next morning. "Your meeting with Nexus Technologies is in 90 minutes. With current traffic conditions, you should leave in 45 minutes."

I blinked at the ceiling, momentarily disoriented by the light. I had not set an alarm; at least, I did not remember doing so. Only then did it dawn on me that the previous day, I had enabled the calendar integration feature on my phone while distracted by an email. The system had scanned my calendar, identified the early morning meeting, calculated the travel time from my location based on historical patterns and current traffic data and woken me accordingly[43].

My first reaction was one of gratitude and shock. I had indeed forgotten to set an alarm, and without this nudge, I would have missed a crucial meeting. My second reaction, as I swung my legs over the side of the bed, was a slight chill unrelated to the room's temperature. It was the realization of how much my movements were being monitored and subtly guided. It reminded me of Dr. Theia's sharing from the other day: technology that worked at the edge of human awareness, subtly making decisions on my behalf based on information I did not provide. Helpful? Without a doubt. Yet, it was also unsettling in its quiet competence[40]. Underlying much of this seamless functionality was the Internet of Things (IoT), where connected devices constantly exchanged data to support ambient decision-making[50].

In the shower, I began to contemplate the history of these supportive systems. The term "ambient intelligence" was coined in the late '90s by Eli Zelkha at Palo Alto Ventures, envisioning a world where technology would be embedded into everyday objects that are context-aware, personalized and adaptive[2,49]. However, the concept had much deeper roots, stretching back through each industrial revolution, each wave representing a step further into the background of human awareness.

I thought about my grandfather's stories of rural electrification in the 1930s: how the simple act of flipping a switch to produce light had seemed miraculous to people who were accustomed to oil lamps and candles. The switch itself was a marvel of interactive design: a direct, physical manipulation yielding an immediate, powerful result. It requires conscious action and a deliberate choice to engage with the electrical system.

Within the passing of a generation, that same light switch had become invisible in daily life, noticed only when it failed to function. The revolution was not the bulb but the interface, the switch, that made complex electrical power use both accessible and controllable by anyone. This was the first step towards seamlessly embedding technology into our lives[28]. The telephone followed a similar pattern, representing the Second Industrial Revolution's focus on communication and interconnectedness.

My grandmother described her family's first rotary phone and how the neighbors gathered to witness the marvel of hearing a distant voice through the receiver. She delightfully demonstrated the deliberate, circular motion of dialing the numbers – a conscious interaction demanding attention, precision, and memory – illustrating how such technology became ingrained over time. Each turn of the dial was a physical command sent down the line to the operator. The technology was tangible, and the interaction was explicit.

During my childhood, the push-button phone simplified interaction, and the cordless phone had already begun to untether communication from a fixed location. My smartphone now connects me instantly to anyone, anywhere, often anticipating whom I might want to call based on my habits. The old methods of dialing may have been forgotten and replaced by voice commands or predictive suggestions. The technology itself had receded further into the background, unseen but used by everyone[48].

The Digital Revolution seems to have accelerated this pattern of subdued acceptance of new technology use. I remembered my first computer; it required a conscious effort to learn commands, deliberate interaction with a keyboard and mouse, and awareness of the machine as a distinct entity. We spoke of "getting on the computer" as a discrete activity. Today, computation no longer announces itself as it once did. Interfaces are increasingly capable of interpreting speech, gestures, and contextual cues, creating experiences so fluid that they often pass below the threshold of conscious attention. What once commanded our attention as a distinct tool now blends into our surroundings, coexisting with us as an accepted part of our environment. It looks that technology is becoming ambient, operating at the bounds of our awareness rather than demanding center stage[46].

As I was dressing up for the day, I wondered if the upcoming Ive-Altman device would follow the same trajectory – from marvel to mundane. The rumored details suggested something that was designed from the outset to be unobtrusive and to enhance rather than interrupt daily life. Unlike earlier technological revolutions that started with conscious interaction before fading into the background, this new device seemed to become ambient from its inception[20]. This new device is also rumored to leverage neuromorphic computing, a brain-inspired approach that processes sensory data with extreme energy efficiency, enabling more sophisticated on-device intelligence without a constant need for cloud connectivity[15,16].

As I walked to the kitchen, I began mentally listing the ambient systems I interacted with daily, often without conscious notice. I noticed that my smart thermostat had adjusted the temperature based on my movement patterns[13,39]. My refrigerator has compiled a shopping list based on its internal cameras and my consumption habits. My news app had curated articles based on my reading history and current events that it deemed relevant based on my interests. Each system, on its own, seemed benign yet helpful; collectively, they represented a profound shift in the role of technology in my life. I was no longer picking up tools and setting them down at will; instead, I seemed to live in an environment that continuously sensed, analyzed and responded to my presence[47]. This interconnectedness seems to be further enhanced by the rise of multimodal ambient intelligence, where systems integrate various sensing modalities – visual, audio, thermal, and even olfactory – to create a more comprehensive and nuanced understanding of the environment and its occupants[1].

As I walked over to the front door, it unlocked on its own, seemingly triggered by the smartphone tucked in my pocket[38]. A security camera above quietly recorded my exit, requiring no effort on my part[36,50,51]. These conveniences have gradually woven themselves into my everyday life. One device at a time, they removed small hassles until, before I knew it, I was living in a seamless web of ambient intelligence. This concept now extends to larger systems, such as smart homes and city infrastructure, which autonomously adjust energy usage and respond to environmental shifts, thereby advancing climate adaptation and sustainability goals[21,23].

I could not help but think of Alura, my elderly neighbor. She is 82 years old, a widower, and lives independently, thanks to a smart care setup her children installed last year. It quietly tracks her movements, sleep quality, medication intake and even changes in her gait, looking for vital signals that might hint at fall risks. Remarkably, it flagged a possible urinary tract infection based on how often she visited the bathroom and the subtle change over a few days, well before she noticed any symptoms herself[6,27]. I came to learn that this system likely uses federated learning, a method that allows devices to improve by learning locally, keeping private data on-site, and protecting user privacy[12,31].

For Alura, this quiet technology is not just helpful; it is a form of freedom. This allows her to live alone safely, providing peace of mind to both her and her family[30]. When I asked her if she found it invasive, she chuckled and said, "Honey, at my age, I welcome anything that keeps an eye on me without making me feel helpless. It does not fuss like my daughter does. It just silently watches out for me."

Her response made me reflect on how technology has supported elder care over the years. Before telephones became common, families relied on letters or in-person visits to check on their loved ones. The phone changed this, making regular updates quick and easy. Ambient intelligence is advancing that concept, delivering constant, unobtrusive monitoring without the need for direct involvement from anyone[18]. However, the extent to which people accept such technologies can vary widely. Culture, privacy values and historical experiences with surveillance shape how societies react to ambient systems[22].

As I picked up my keys and walked toward the door, a thought lingered: perhaps our relationship with these invisible systems hinges on whether we see them as tools for autonomy or as forms of control[17]. For Alura, they seem to empower her to speak out. They provided her with space and safety without dependency on others. I was not entirely sure yet. As these systems become more integrated into our lives, ethical questions arise. This has led to the development of frameworks for ambient intelligence ethics, emphasizing human agency, openness and accountability[21].

Just then, my phone buzzed: "Leave now to reach Nexus Technologies on time. Heavy traffic detected on your regular route." I stepped outside, still reflecting on Dr. Theia's comments the day before. I was on my way to meet a potential client seeking advice on "ambient workplace solutions" – a coincidence that felt almost too perfect. Or maybe, I thought, smirking slightly, it was just a well-timed nudge from some attentive algorithm.

The Business of Invisibility - Ambient Intelligence in the Workplace

The Nexus Technologies compound comprised of three sleek modern buildings that were seamlessly connected by glass walkways. As I neared the main entrance, the doors glided open without needing a touch[32]. Inside, a gentle chime sounded and a receptionist greeted me with a friendly smile, even though we had never met before.

“Good morning!”, she said warmly. “I think you must be here for the 9:30 meeting. Would you like some coffee while you wait? The team will be with you shortly.” I nodded in affirmation, pleasantly surprised by the smooth reception. “Coffee would be great, thanks.” She gestured toward a vending machine in the corner. “Please, help yourself. It is tuned to guest preferences.”

I walked over, intrigued by the scene. The machine had no visible buttons, only a glossy surface that lit up as I approached. Before I could make a choice, the screen displayed: “Preparing: Black coffee, medium strength, no sugar.” My usual order. The machine whirred gently, delivering a fresh cup. I took a cautious sip – it was just right: balanced, smooth, familiar.

“How did it know?” I asked the receptionist about the matter. She smiled knowingly and said, “It recognized your details from the calendar invite on your phone and matched them with publicly accessible preference data. We make use of this data to make guests feel more at home”[11]. I nodded, impressed, not wanting to show that I felt slightly uneasy about the way my gadgets and data were accessed. Sure, my coffee habits were not classified, but I could not remember ever providing that information in a way that would be so easily found.

That brief encounter reminded me of how workplace hospitality has changed across industrial eras. Back in the early days of industrialization, factory workers were handed the same basic cup of tea – uniform and impersonal, much like the production lines they worked on. As offices paved the way, secretaries started to focus on personalizing hospitality by recalling repeat visitors' preferences, a gesture of memory and care. The advent of the digital age has allowed users to select their drinks via touchscreens, which is a better choice than direct interaction. Currently, ambient intelligence has gone beyond all these and started anticipating what we want before we ask, crafting a subtle but surprisingly intuitive experience. This move from deliberate input to passive prediction is one of the defining traits of mature ambient systems[22].

My conversation with the Nexus team was based on this insight. They were designing an integrated ecosystem of ambient tools that supported both productivity and all round well-being in the workplace. One feature that stood out was their adaptive lighting system. It self-adjusted not only to the brightness of the room but also to individual users' preferences and natural daily rhythms, aiming to improve concentration and ease eye strain. "We are not just conserving power," said David, the lead engineer. "We are building workspaces that actively nurture mental clarity and emotional needs. In our pilot implementations, we have seen promising improvements in output and noticeable drop in stress levels." This support reflects a more advanced stage of ambient intelligence as technology becomes aware, responsive and aligned with human needs[14].

Equally compelling was their smart meeting assistant. Far from just recording conversations, it analyzed facial expressions, tone of voice and even biometric data from wearables, with consent, to read the emotional temperature of a room. "If someone zones out or tension spikes, it can suggest a pause or rephrase something that's unclear," David explained. "It is not about taking over but about making communication smoother." Using multiple data inputs to better understand human interaction is a powerful example of ambient intelligence moving toward true contextual awareness[2].

They also showed me how their system could predict when office equipment would likely fail. By collecting sensor data in real time and by applying machine learning algorithms, they could predict breakdowns even before they happened. "We have reduced equipment downtime by nearly a third," David noted proudly. "This is what we mean by a self-correcting, intelligent environment." Creating such resilient systems marks a big shift in workplace technology – one where the environment itself can learn and adapt continuously[7].

Naturally, our conversation also turned toward the ethical aspects. "How do you maintain that balance – between helpful and overbearing?" I asked, still thinking about how the coffee machine anticipated my preferences. "And how do you avoid crossing the line into surveillance?" David nodded. "That is the big question. We believe in complete transparency. Users need to know what data are being gathered, and they can opt out at any time. We also carry out regular audits and have a dedicated ethics board that oversees every new implementation." You ensure that a user has autonomy, and ethical oversight is crucial for responsible adoption, especially in places where trust matters most, such as the workplace[3].

As I ended my visit after sharing my views on the likely areas that they could refine further, one thing was clearly evident: ambient intelligence is not just about adding convenience to our homes. It represents a fundamental shift in how we relate to technology in both our personal and professional lives. What truly makes this technology valuable is not how advanced it is, but how carefully and ethically it is crafted to interact and support. When implemented with care, it blends into the background, enhancing our daily experiences without interfering with our independence or privacy. The real breakthrough lies in designing and building systems that are not only smart but also human at their core – quietly helpful, respectful and almost invisible.

The Ethical Labyrinth - Navigating the Invisible Revolution

Returning home from Nexus Technologies, my mind was spinning with various thoughts, energized by what I had noticed. Their seamless ambient solutions were undeniably impressive, yet they brought long-standing ethical questions to the surface, questions that had been echoing in my mind since Dr. Theia's recent interview. As technology becomes quieter and more integrated, who remains accountable? How can we avoid its misuse? What happens to human values when algorithms silently make our choices?

These questions led me into the increasingly urgent world of ethics in ambient intelligence. It did not take long for me to understand that this was not just an academic debate; it was a pressing issue for society as a whole. As governments, businesses and advocacy groups attempt to steer the development of ambient intelligence responsibly, they are constantly trying to balance its clear advantages – such as improved efficiency, safety and convenience – with its equally significant drawbacks, including the erosion of privacy, biased decision-making and the potential loss of personal agency[9].

A major ethical point to consider is what scholars describe as "algorithmic opacity." These systems often rely on complex or proprietary algorithms, making it extremely difficult to trace how decisions are made such as who gets approved for a loan or offered a job. In areas where the stakes are high, this lack of transparency can reinforce social inequality. In response, new ethical standards advocate for explainable AI (XAI), which aims to make the inner workings of these systems comprehensible and supports the use of third-party audits to catch and minimize bias[52].

Data privacy, unsurprisingly, is another major concern. Ambient systems gather vast amounts of information – everything from how we move and speak to our biometric signals and our shopping routines. While this enables tailored, proactive services, it also opens the door to surveillance, leaks and unauthorized sharing. Regulations like the GDPR in Europe and CCPA in California are helping give users more say over their data, but ambient systems often operate in subtle, pervasive ways that challenge both compliance and enforcement[21].

At the heart of it all is the question of human agency itself. If systems always guess what we want, do we slowly lose the habit of making choices for ourselves? If a thermostat adjusts before we feel cold, or if we are redirected without warning by smart navigation, are we drifting into passive acceptance? Critics argue that such "nudging" can chip away at our independence over time[5]. Supporters, meanwhile, liken it to tools like calculators, freeing us from routine tasks so we can focus on more meaningful work. The real task is to design systems that support rather than supplant our decisions.

My exploration also uncovered global inequalities in how ambient technology is adopted. While developed nations debate privacy and bias, others are still working to establish a basic digital infrastructure. This quiet technological revolution risks deepening the digital divide; some communities reap the benefits while others fall further behind. Cultural factors also shape how people react to these technologies; in some places, ever-present sensing is embraced as efficient, while elsewhere, it is met with caution or suspicion due to past surveillance or differing views on privacy[21].

For weeks, I immersed myself in these topics, reading research, analyzing policy papers, and talking with ethicists, engineers, and people who deliberately live off the grid. One thing was obvious: there are no simple answers to this question. The ethics of ambient intelligence is a constantly evolving field, one that demands continued dialogue, flexible regulation and a firm commitment to keeping humans at the center of design.

Dr. Theia's words seem to coin this accurately: “Intelligence itself is becoming ambient – everywhere, yet nowhere to be seen.” While invisibility is key to a seamless user experience, it raises serious questions about control and privacy. As these technologies blend into our surroundings, always listening and adapting, how do we stay in charge of our lives and our data? The old model of privacy, clear permissions and defined boundaries, no longer fully applies in this new ambient world[3].

Smart homes were once places of solitude and privacy. They are now silent, observant partners. The lights turn on as I walk through a room. My Bluetooth speaker knows which playlist to start at which time of the day and based on my mood. The fridge pings reminders about aging groceries. Each task seems minor, but together, they form a comprehensive picture of how I live. Most of this data is gathered without active consent and it is often fed into systems that learn from and act on it. The concern is not just about what is collected but also about who gets access and how that data is ultimately used.

Bias is another pressing issue. If ambient systems are built to serve people, whose preferences are embedded in them? If the datasets used to train these systems are limited or skewed, then entire groups may find themselves misunderstood or excluded. A smart home trained mostly on the habits of one demographic may miss the mark for others, particularly those with different cultural practices or accessibility needs[22].

The challenge is that ambient technology often works silently. When bias slips in, it is difficult to detect and even more difficult to trace. That is why ethical governance is so crucial. Collaborative frameworks that involve technologists, ethicists, regulators and the public are being developed to ensure transparency (making systems understandable), accountability (defining who is responsible) and human oversight (keeping users in control)[21].

This is not a hypothetical debate. These systems are already influencing how we behave, connect and think. The opportunity is immense but so are the stakes. If we want ambient intelligence to serve us well, we must be deliberate in how we build it. This means constant reflection, meaningful dialogue, and above all, an insistence on systems that are ethical, inclusive, and deeply human.

The Human Element - Ambient Intelligence in Healthcare and Beyond

A few weeks later, I was sitting in a clinical waiting room, accompanying my mother-in-law, Alura, for her routine check-up. The setting I noticed in that waiting room was a far cry from the advanced and polished feel of the Nexus campus. On the contrary, ambient intelligence was quietly at work even there.

At check-in, a compact device embedded in the counter scanned her health card. A gentle voice followed: “Hi Alura! Your 10:30 AM appointment with Dr. Chen has been confirmed. Please proceed to waiting area B. Your vital signs will be recorded automatically.” As she walked through an archway, I noticed a small green light blink[29].

“What was that?” I asked her softly. “Oh, it’s just the clinic’s new system,” she replied, settling into her seat. “It reads my vital signs as I walk in. No need for that age-old and uncomfortable blood pressure cuff anymore”[25]. I was struck by how seamlessly ambient intelligence had extended into the medical setting, beyond the at-home care system Alura already relied on.

A while later during her appointment, I noticed Dr. Chen scrolling through a tablet showing real-time metrics, past trends and predictive health alerts. The software even identified possible drug conflicts and proposed custom preventative care strategies based on Alura’s genetics and lifestyle data[44].

"It is like having a constant intelligent assistant," Dr. Chen remarked when she saw my interest. "This allows us to anticipate problems much earlier without waiting for symptoms to appear. Using multimodal ambient intelligence, we combine inputs from wearables, smart home devices and even external environmental data to create a full picture of each patient's health, inside and outside the clinic"[34].

Still, this level of passive data collection sparked some familiar concerns around privacy. Dr. Chen was quick to reassure me: all data is encrypted, anonymized and fully controlled by patients. "The aim is not surveillance, it is the support," she said. "We are building a system that promotes health quietly and respectfully." This mirrors the core values in ambient intelligence ethics guidelines now being created, which emphasize on user control, openness and responsible system design[21].

Once I began noticing it, I saw ambient intelligence popping up in all sorts of places. On my commute, traffic signals adjust themselves based on live traffic patterns to reduce delays[46]. In local parks, environmental sensors tracked air quality and noise, contributing to better urban planning[21]. Even retail stores had adopted it, fine-tuning product placement and customizing shopping experiences without the need for customers to touch a screen or speak to staff[11]. Increasingly, consumer technologies such as drones are also being adapted for similar ambient purposes, capturing data and enhancing security or logistics while blending seamlessly into daily life[35].

The RAS Effect - Ambient Intelligence in My Own Backyard

Upon returning to work, I began to notice signs of ambient intelligence everywhere. It reminded me of the Reticular Activating System (RAS) – that phenomenon where, something new enters your awareness and suddenly shows up all around you. Take our building's HVAC system, for instance. I initially ignored it as just a regular upgrade but now I realized it was a textbook case of ambient intelligence aiding climate resilience, where infrastructure responds in real time to both human needs and environmental demands[21].

Our IT team was exploring federated learning for our cybersecurity protocols. Instead of funnelling all network data to a central hub for threat detection, each device was trained to spot irregular patterns locally and share only summary insights. This decentralized approach improved system security while greatly minimizing privacy risks[12].

Even our internal messaging platform which I always thought was clunky and outdated suddenly started to feel smarter. I started noticing that it now offered suggestions for potential collaborators, condensed long email chains and even drafted replies for simpler queries. It was behaving like a low-key digital assistant, quietly learning from my habits and shaping itself around how I work[11].

These experiences allowed me to reflect on how different cultures might perceive this shift. In some places, the notion of ever-present, unseen technology might raise concerns about control and monitoring while in others, it could be welcomed as a natural way to boost collective productivity and ease daily routines. Conversations with Alura and my time at Nexus Technologies brought out as to just how crucial it is to design ambient systems with cultural awareness and user trust at the forefront[22].

The Future Unveiled - A Glimpse of the 'Third Core Device'

As the time passed by, rumours about the much anticipated "third core device" from Jony Ive and Sam Altman only grew louder. Hints and leaks described something ground-breaking; of an ambient companion that would quietly integrate into everyday routines without needing constant interaction from the users. It was being referred to as "proactive AI", something that could anticipate your needs, manage your information and support interactions so naturally that it is seen more like an extension of thought than a separate gadget[20].

Then, unexpectedly, an invitation landed in my inbox – an exclusive preview of the "io" device, co-hosted by OpenAI and Jony Ive's renowned design studio. My excitement surged. This felt like the endpoint of everything I had been exploring, the chance to step into the next phase of the ambient intelligence journey.

The venue had a calm, minimalist design that mirrored the elegance of the event itself. Jony Ive, poised and composed as ever, appeared on stage beside Sam

Altman. Rather than diving into tech specs or flashy features, they spoke about the purpose behind the product, a commitment to technology that honoured human attention and enriched daily life, rather than stealing focus. They explained that the device's core was built on neuromorphic computing, allowing for highly efficient, real-time processing of sensory inputs directly on the device. This enabled contextual responsiveness without any dependence on cloud-based systems[15].

When they finally revealed the device, it looked modest – nothing flashy but just a smooth, pebble-shaped object that sat comfortably in the hand. It had no screen, no buttons, no glaring indicators. Its strength was in its quiet intelligence: the ability to interpret context, learn from the environment and respond subtly and meaningfully. It embodied the purest vision of ambient intelligence – technology that blends in so completely, you only notice what it empowers you to do[40].

As I held the device, with its sleek and cool surface, in my palm, I felt as though I was holding a symbol of everything this "invisible revolution" stood for. This was the evolution from the light switch to intuitive, adaptive intelligence. Glancing around the room at others who were equally absorbed, I felt we were all witnessing a pivotal shift in our connection to technology. Intelligence was no longer something we operated; it was becoming part of the fabric of everyday life.

What had started as a passing interest had now become something deeper. I began to recognize that ambient intelligence was not just the next tech wave; it represented a profound redefinition of how we live with technology. This silent revolution was already rewriting the rules in our homes, workplaces and personal lives. The experiences I had gathered, like Alura's newfound autonomy or my own discomfort with predictive algorithms, made it clear how profoundly these systems touched us.

I also began viewing broader developments differently. Concepts I had once seen as abstract – smart cities, environmental sensing, autonomous traffic systems[9], they now looked like logical next steps. Health technologies, once distant dreams in medical journals, were now wearable and in real-time, offer insights and predictions tailored to each individual. Education too was evolving through platforms that adapted learning materials based on each student's pace and needs[43].

With understanding came responsibility. The ethical issues – privacy, bias, autonomy and access – were no longer hypothetical. They were present, urgent and in need of collective action. This invisible shift in how we interact with technology was not inherently good or bad. The outcomes would be shaped by the choices we made: how we built these systems, who governed them and what principles guided their design.

I recalled Dr. Theia's reflection on historical technologies – the light bulb, the telephone and the computer. They all began as novelties and later faded into the background. Ambient intelligence was on the same path, but its stealth made it more powerful and more ethically fraught. Because it operates in the background, we must be more careful to ensure it remains aligned with our values. Passive acceptance was not an option, we needed to question, critique and ensure accountability.

This exploration had transformed how I engaged with technology. I became a more intentional user and felt a growing desire to contribute to the conversation, to help steer the future of AI in a direction that revolves around human dignity and well-being.

Now, as I sit at my desk finishing this reflection, the lights around me dim slightly, my smart speaker adjusting the ambiance for the evening. My phone, resting quietly, has already reduced its brightness. These actions might seem insignificant, but they are now part of my awareness. I notice them. I understand them. And I realize that the invisible revolution is not just altering our surroundings, it is reshaping our inner world, our expectations and how we imagine the road ahead.

An Invisible Revolution: A Personal Reflection and the Next Wave

My sojourn into the world of ambient intelligence began unconsciously. It all started with a news ticker and a casual morning broadcast that I chanced to notice. But what followed was a profound exploration of how technology is quietly reshaping our lives in ways beyond one's comprehension – subtle and significant. From the subtle adjustments in my smart home to the sophisticated systems at Nexus Technologies and the ambient care that empowered Alura her independence, I came to realize that we are in the middle of an invisible revolution, one not declared with any fanfare, but is unfolding through imperceptible shifts all around us.

This revolution is ambient intelligence – of systems that integrate seamlessly into our environments, sensing, anticipating and responding to our needs without requiring our attention. From the echoes of the Industrial Revolutions to today's neuromorphic computing and multimodal AI, the evolution of ambient intelligence reflects our relentless pursuit of convenience, efficiency and control[15,21].

The much anticipated "third core device" from Jony Ive and Sam Altman embodies this shift. Designed to reduce screen dependency while maintaining ambient awareness, it reportedly leverages neuromorphic computing – a brain-inspired approach that processes data with extreme energy efficiency, enabling sophisticated on-device intelligence without reliance on the cloud[20,40,41]. This technology does not just respond; its intuitive, predicting needs before they are expressed. This is the essence of ambient intelligence.

Similarly, multimodal ambient systems that integrate visual, audio, thermal and even olfactory sensing provide richer contextual awareness. These systems can personalize and optimize energy use, support elderly care and adapt city infrastructure in real-time – whether adjusting traffic lights, monitoring air quality or regulating building temperatures[21,26,34].

The impact spans across domains – homes, workplaces, hospitals and cities. At Nexus Technologies, ambient systems anticipated employee needs, optimized lighting and temperature, predicted equipment failures and even facilitated communication through digital assistants[11,39]. In healthcare, Alura's check-up revealed how ambient systems collected vitals unobtrusively and analyzed them alongside personal health history and environmental data to recommend preventive care[25,44].

Yet, as these systems become more pervasive and capable, the responsibilities grow equally profound. The qualities that make ambient intelligence powerful – its invisibility, predictive capability and seamless integration – also pose complex challenges around privacy, autonomy and fairness[3,22].

The constant collection and analysis of personal data, even when anonymized or aggregated, creates vulnerabilities. Federated learning offers some hope – allowing devices to learn from local data without transmitting raw information to central servers[12]. But even this raises questions: Who controls the algorithms? Who sets the thresholds of intervention? What if the models misinterpret the context or reinforce biases?

Indeed, algorithmic bias can be amplified when ambient systems misread human behavior, particularly across diverse cultures, abilities, or socio-economic backgrounds[7]. The key lies in embedding ethical principles from the ground up: transparency, accountability and human oversight must not be after-thoughts but foundational design imperatives[21].

Equity must also be central to our vision. In some parts of the world, ambient systems enhance daily life and autonomy while in other parts, they may be viewed with suspicion, shaped by histories of surveillance or differing expectations around privacy. A one-size-fits-all approach will not work. Cultural sensitivity, inclusive design and global cooperation are essential for ethical adoption[17,22].

As I reflect on this journey, I see not just the awe-inspiring potential of ambient intelligence but also the urgent need for a shared responsibility. This revolution is not merely technological; it is social, ethical and deeply human. Ambient intelligence can enhance our well-being, productivity, independence and even help combat climate change through intelligent energy management – only if it is designed to empower rather than control, to support rather than surveil.

The future is not waiting, it is already unfolding quietly everywhere around and within us. From the smart light that adjusts before we notice the darkness to the device that suggests an alternate route before we sense traffic, ambient AI is becoming an impeccable part within the fabric of our lives. We are no longer mere users of any tools that make our tasks easier; we are participants and contributors in an ambient ecosystem.

The challenge and the opportunity is ours to decide and set course – to ensure that this invisible revolution aligns with our values, reflects our diversity, respects our rights and uplifts our humanity. The conversation has only just begun and it is one that we must all actively engage in. For the revolution of ambient intelligence is not just about machines becoming smarter, it is about us becoming wiser in how we design, deploy and live with them.

Tomorrow's quiet symphony awaits our beckoning - let us compose it with utmost reason, compassion, insight and empathy.

References

1. Adeli, E. (2025, May 7). Ambient intelligence, human impact. Stanford HAI. https://hai.stanford.edu/news/ambient-intelligence-human-impact

2. Aggarwal, S. (2025, March 17). Ambient intelligence: Next step for artificial intelligence. TechAhead. https://www.techaheadcorp.com/blog/ambient-intelligence-next-step-for-artificial-intelligence/

3. AI Ethics Journal. (n.d.). Retrieved June 14, 2025, from https://www.aiethicsjournal.org/

4. Amigoni, F., Gatti, N., Pinciroli, C., & Roveri, M. (2005, January 31). What planner for ambient intelligence applications? IEEE Transactions on Systems, Man and Cybernetics – Part A: Systems and Humans, 35(1), 7–21. https://ieeexplore.ieee.org/document/1369341

5. Bartman, M. (2022, April 22). The Ethics of AI-Powered Climate Nudging – How Much AI Should We Use to Save the Planet? Sustainability, 14(9), 5153. https://doi.org/10.3390/su14095153

6. Capstick, A., Palermo, F., Zakka, K., Lloyd, N. F., Walsh, C., Cui, T., ... Barnaghi, P. (2024, January 13). Digital remote monitoring for screening and early detection of urinary tract infections. npj Digital Medicine, 7(11). https://doi.org/10.1038/s41746-023-00995-5

7. Cook, D. J., Augusto, J. C., & Jakkula, V. R. (2009, August). Ambient intelligence: Technologies, applications and opportunities. Pervasive and Mobile Computing, 5(4), 277–298. https://doi.org/10.1016/j.pmcj.2009.04.001

8. Crowley, J. L., & Coutaz, J. (2015, October 30). An ecological view of smart home technologies. In B. de Ruyter, A. Kameas, P. Chatzimisios, & I. Mavrommati (Eds.), Ambient Intelligence (Lecture Notes in Computer Science, Vol. 9425, pp. 7–21). Springer. https://doi.org/10.1007/978-3-319-26005-1_1

9. Deloitte Insights. (2015, January). Ambient computing: Putting the Internet of Things to work. Deloitte Tech Trends. https://www2.deloitte.com/content/www/us/en/insights/focus/tech-trends/2015/tech-trends-2015-ambient-computing.html

10. Forbes Technology Council. (2022a, April 11). Two trends in tech 2022 – and one that should be. Forbes. https://www.forbes.com/councils/forbestechcouncil/2022/04/11/two-trends-in-tech-2022-and-one-that-should-be/

11. Forbes Technology Council. (2022b, November 21). Ambient computing is at the heart of the frictionless economy. Forbes. https://www.forbes.com/sites/forbestechcouncil/2022/11/21/ambient-computing-is-at-the-heart-of-the-frictionless-economy/

12. Google AI Blog. (2023, March 2). Distributed differential privacy for federated learning. Google Research. https://research.google/blog/distributed-differential-privacy-for-federated-learning/

13. Han, X. Q., Gao, Z. F., Wang, X. D., Ouyang, Z., Guo, P. J., & Lu, Z. Y. (2025, June 4). HTSC-2025: A Benchmark Dataset of Ambient-Pressure High-Temperature Superconductors for AI-Driven Critical Temperature Prediction [Preprint]. arXiv. https://arxiv.org/html/2506.03837v1

14. Horr, Y. A., Arif, M., Kaushik, A., Mazroei, A., Katafygiotou, M., & Elsarrag, E. (2016, August 15). Occupant productivity

and office indoor environment quality: A review. Building and Environment, 105, 369–389. https://doi.org/10.1016/j.buildenv.2016.06.001

15. IBM Research. (2024, October 24). The chips of tomorrow may well take inspiration from the architecture of our brains. https://research.ibm.com/blog/what-is-neuromorphic-or-brain-inspired-computing

16. Innatera. (2025, January 7). Innatera showcases revolutionary neuromorphic processor enabling next-generation ambient intelligence at CES 2025. https://innatera.com/news/innatera-showcases-revolutionary-neuromorphic-processor-enabling-next-generation-ambient-intelligence-at-ces-2025

17. Iwashita, M., Ishida, K., & Ishikawa, M. (2021, August 10). Effect of user personality on efficacy of a mental support system based on ambient intelligence: A case study. Frontiers in Computer Science. 3:702069. https://doi.org/10.3389/fcomp.2021.702069

18. Liao, Y., Vitak, J., Kumar, P., Zimmer, M., & Kritikos, K. (2019, March 13). Understanding the role of privacy and trust in intelligent personal assistant adoption. Information in Contemporary Society (pp. 102–113). Springer. https://doi.org/10.1007/978-3-030-15742-5_9

19. Liu, J., Lin, Z., Wu, J., & Venkatesh, V. (2009, December). uWave: Accelerometer-based personalized gesture recognition and its applications. Pervasive and Mobile Computing, 5(5), 496–508. https://doi.org/10.1016/j.pmcj.2009.04.001

20. MacRumors. (2025, May 22). Jony Ive's AI product "third core device" after MacBook and iPhone. https://www.macrumors.com/2025/05/22/jony-ive-openai-product-third-core-device/

21. Marwala, T. (2025, May 12). Why the need for governing ambient intelligence has never been more urgent. United Nations University. https://unu.edu/article/why-need-

governing-ambient-intelligence-has-never-been-more-urgent

22. MIT Technology Review. (2024, February 15). Responsible technology use in the AI age. https://www.technologyreview.com/2024/02/15/1087815/responsible-technology-use-in-the-ai-age/

23. Nguyen, T. T. H., Nguyen, P. T. L., Wachowicz, M., & Cao, H. (2024, September). MACeIP: A multimodal ambient context-enriched intelligence platform in smart cities [Preprint]. arXiv. https://arxiv.org/pdf/2409.15243.pdf

24. Okomayin, A., & Ige, T. (2024, September). Ambient technology & intelligence [Preprint]. arXiv. https://arxiv.org/abs/2305.10726

25. Patel, N. R., Lacher, C. R., Huang, A. Y., Kolomeyer, A., Bavinger, J. C., Carroll, R. M., Kim, B. J., & Tsui, J. C. (2025, May 23). Evaluating the application of artificial intelligence and ambient listening to generate medical notes in vitreoretinal clinic encounters. Dove Press, Ophthalmology and Therapeutics. https://www.dovepress.com/evaluating-the-application-of-artificial-intelligence-and-ambient-list-peer-reviewed-fulltext-article-OPTH

26. Philips Hue Developer News. (2024, May). Connected energy consumption study. https://developers.meethue.com/connected-energy-consumption-study/

27. PubMed. (2022). Internet of Medical Things (IoMT)-based smart healthcare system: Trends and progress. Retrieved from https://pubmed.ncbi.nlm.nih.gov/35880061/

28. Reddy, T. A. S. (2022, October). Ambient computing: The integration of technology into our daily lives. Online Scientific Research. https://www.onlinescientificresearch.com/articles/ambient-computing-the-integration-of-technology-into-our-daily-lives.pdf

29. Remagnino, P., & Foresti, G. L. (2004, December 20). Ambient intelligence: A new multidisciplinary paradigm.

IEEE Transactions on Systems, Man and Cybernetics – Part A, 35(1), 1–6. https://doi.org/10.1109/TSMCA.2004.838456

30. Remagnino, P., Foresti, G. L., & Ellis, T. (2005). Ambient intelligence: A novel paradigm. Springer. https://doi.org/10.1007/b100343

31. Shawkat, M., Ali, Z. H., Salem, M., & El-desoky, A. (2025, April 23). A robust and personalized privacy-preserving approach for adaptive clustered federated distillation. Scientific Reports, 15(4), Article 96468. https://doi.org/10.1038/s41598-025-96468-8

32. Shukla, S., Yang, J., Tan, R., Wu, Q., & Gao, J. (2025, February 25). Magma: A foundation model for multimodal AI agents across digital and physical worlds. Microsoft Research. https://www.microsoft.com/en-us/research/blog/magma-a-foundation-model-for-multimodal-ai-agents-across-digital-and-physical-worlds/

33. Signify. (2025, January 7). Philips Hue unveils next-gen AI-powered smart lighting and home security innovations. https://www.signify.com/global/our-company/news/press-releases/2025/20250107-philips-hue-unveils-next-gen-ai-powered-smart-lighting-and-smart-home-security-innovations

34. Stanford HAI. (2025, January 27). Stanford's multimodal AI model advances personalized cancer care. https://hai.stanford.edu/news/stanfords-multimodal-ai-model-advances-personalized-cancer-care

35. Stephany, F. (2024, February 27). 2023: The Year AI Redefined Work, Skills, and the Future of Employment. Oxford Internet Institute. https://www.oii.ox.ac.uk/news-events/2023-the-year-ai-redefined-work-skills-and-the-future-of-employment/

36. TechRadar. (2025a, March). The best drone 2025: Top flying cameras for all budgets. https://www.techradar.com/news/best-drones

37. TechRadar. (2025b, April). Ring cameras used to spy on you, is it safe to use smart devices?

https://www.techradar.com/computing/cyber-security/ring-cameras-used-to-spy-on-youis-it-safe-to-use-smart-devices

38. TechRadar. (2025c, February). The best smart thermostat 2025: Save money with smart energy tech. https://www.techradar.com/news/best-smart-thermostat

39. TechRadar. (2025d, March). 5 best smart locks (2025), tested and reviewed. https://www.techradar.com/news/best-smart-locks

40. TechRadar (2025e, February 16). 5 massive AI trends I'm looking out for in 2025. https://www.techradar.com/computing/artificial-intelligence/ai-in-2025-whats-coming-next-and-what-matters

41. The Verge. (2025a, May 22). Jony Ive's AI gadget rumoured to be 'slightly larger' than Humane's AI pin. https://www.theverge.com/news/672533/jony-ive-sam-altman-ai-device-ipod-shuffle-ai-pin

42. The Verge (2025b, May 22). Details leak about Jony Ive's new 'screen-free' OpenAI device. https://www.theverge.com/news/672357/openai-ai-device-sam-altman-jony-ive

43. Ulanoff, L. (2023, December 27). The biggest tech trends to watch in 2024: AI, Vision Pro, EVs and more. TechRadar. https://www.techradar.com/tech/ai-vision-pro-evs-and-more-know-these-10-tech-trends-and-be-the-smartest-person-in-the-room-in-2024

44. UNESCO. (2024, September 26). Recommendation on the ethics of artificial intelligence. https://www.unesco.org/en/articles/recommendation-ethics-artificial-intelligence

45. Wang, Y., Yalcin, A., & Vandeweerd, C. (2020, March 4). Health and wellness monitoring using ambient sensor networks. Journal of Ambient Intelligence and Smart Environments. 2020;12(2):139-151. https://doi.org/10.3233/AIS-200553

46. Weiser, M. (1991). The computer for the 21st century. Scientific American, 265(3), 94–104. https://www.cs.cmu.edu/~jasonh/courses/ubicomp-sp2007/papers/02-weiser-computer-21st-century.pdf

47. Wikipedia. (2025a). Smart city. https://en.wikipedia.org/wiki/Smart_city

48. Wikipedia. (2025b). Ambient intelligence. https://en.wikipedia.org/wiki/Ambient_intelligence

49. Wikipedia. (2025c, April). Internet of things. https://en.wikipedia.org/wiki/Internet_of_things

50. Wikipedia. (2025d, February). Smart doorbell. https://en.wikipedia.org/wiki/Smart_doorbell

51. Wired. (2017, September 20). Inside the second coming of Nest. Wired. https://www.wired.com/story/inside-the-second-coming-of-nest/

52. Wired (2019, July 18). High-Stakes AI Decisions Need to Be Automatically Audited https://www.wired.com/story/ai-needs-to-be-audited

Afterword

Acknowledging the Architects of Insight

The volume "*Advances Using AI – The Next Wave*" echoes a way of collective thinking and the deep commitment of many people. While the previous epilogue alluded to an overarching narrative of collective purpose and joint effort, it is in this section that we formally acknowledge each author, whose domain expertise and commitment led to this academic endeavor.

We particularly acknowledge the Editors, who managed this project, from inception to completion:

- **Vanamali Somanchi**: Chief editor, and the creative founder of this joint endeavor, whose concept brought together multiple voices.
- **Richard R. Khan**: Co-editor, whose leadership and proposal made this project a book.
- **Tulay Guneysel**: Co-editor, whose contributions and editorial experience maintained a consistency and standard of the book.

We also sincerely thank our esteemed Authors whose serious reflections and involved research are at the core of this volume:

DOI: 10.1201/9781003737803-10

- **Abhay Tewari**: Author of "AI for Rural-Classrooms to Industry-Skilling", for his significant contribution in raising the reach and impact of AI in less-served communities.
- **Jasika Singh**: Author of "Decoding Emotions with AI", for her reflections on the important nuances of the relationship of AI and human emotion.
- **Jitendra Bikram Shah**: Author of "Probabilistic AI: Frameworks for Uncertainty", for his learned pathway through the labyrinth of AI under frameworks of uncertainty.
- **Joshua Lau Boon Wei**: Author of "The Intelligent Journey", for his important reflections on the role, and impact, of AI that continues to change.
- **Partho S. Ghosh**: Author of "Harvesting the Stars" and author of a chapter in "Stamped in Silicon: When Robots Queue at Customs", for his visionary contributions to the ambitious applications of AI.
- **Richard R. Khan**: Author of "Stamped in Silicon: When Robots Queue at Customs", for his valuable commentary on AI's societal integration and ethical implications.
- **Siddharth Hegde**: Author of "Smarter, Faster, Greener: AI's Role in Responsible 6G", for his encouraging commentary on advocating for sustainable AI development.
- **Tulay Guneysel**: Author of "Red Flags in Code: AI and the Future of Auditing", for her valuable exigence to articulate some important ethical issues and questions associated with the future of AI in audit.

- **Vanamali Somanchi**: Author of "The Invisible Revolution", for his intellectually stimulating views on the quiet yet profound changes caused by AI.

Each of these distinguished individuals boldly negotiated challenging career trajectories including, and not limited to, the demanding challenges associated with doctoral research to contribute their expertise and efforts across the volume. The persistent effort embedded in developing the awareness of artificial intelligence, and combined desire to 'reinvent' themselves in artificial intelligence is admirable. This volume illustrates their commitment to and success in joint learning.

Glossary

1. 6G (Sixth-Generation Wireless)

   (Smarter, Faster, Greener: AI's Role in Sustainable 6G, p. 163-182)

   6G is the next generation of wireless technology, which is expected to be deployed in the 2030s. It promises to be significantly faster and more reliable than 5G, with lower latency and higher bandwidth. 6G is expected to enable a new wave of applications and services, including holographic communication, immersive entertainment, and the tactile internet.

2. Affective Computing (Emotion AI)

   (*Decoding Emotions with AI*, p. 45)

   Affective computing enables machines to recognize, interpret, and respond to human emotions. It combines inputs like facial expressions, speech tone, and physiological signals from wearables to estimate mood or stress. These systems can offer prompt support, such as suggesting a break when stress is high. While promising in healthcare and learning, affective computing raises concerns about cultural sensitivity, data privacy, and the risk of over-interpreting subtle human signals.

3. Agentic AI

   (*The Intelligent Journey*, p. 107, 112)

   Agentic AI refers to highly autonomous systems that act on behalf of users, sometimes managing entire processes without direct prompts. In travel, for example, such systems might book flights, re-route itineraries, and handle reimbursements automatically. Their "agent-like" qualities promise convenience but also raise governance questions: how much independence should we allow a machine, and how do we ensure transparency, accountability, and alignment with user intent?

4. Aleatoric Uncertainty

   (*Probabilistic AI: Navigating Uncertainty*, p. 84)

   Aleatoric uncertainty describes randomness built into nature, such as unpredictable raindrop timing or variability in patient responses to treatment. Even with perfect models, this uncertainty stays. In AI, recognizing aleatoric uncertainty means designing systems that withstand randomness, like healthcare models that account for varied patient outcomes. Mistaking it for something fixable can waste resources, while ignoring it can lead to brittle, unreliable systems.

5. Ambient Intelligence (AmI)

   (*The Invisible Revolution*, p. 203-233)

Ambient intelligence describes environments embedded with AI that sense and respond to people invisibly. Lights that brighten as you walk in, thermostats adjusting before you feel cold, or health systems quietly watching vital signs are examples. The power of Ami lies in its invisibility, enabling convenience and safety without demanding attention. Yet its very subtlety creates ethical dilemmas around autonomy, privacy, and ensuring people stay in control of their choices.

6. Anomaly (AI Auditing Context)

(*Red Flags in Code: AI and the Future of Auditing*, p. 188)

An anomaly refers to an unusual or unexpected data pattern flagged by AI systems. It is not by itself evidence of fraud or error but rather a signal that further professional investigation is needed. Anomalies may result from legitimate business events, irregularities, or system noise, and therefore require human judgment to interpret appropriately.

7. Artificial Intelligence (AI)

(*AI for Rural-Classrooms to Industry-Skilling*, p. 3, 29; Decoding Emotions with AI, p. 41, 45; *Probabilistic AI: Navigating Uncertainty*, p. 77, 83; *The Intelligent Journey*, p. 103; *Harvesting the Stars*, p. 124-138; *Smarter, Faster, Greener: AI's Role in Sustainable 6G*, p. 181; *Red Flags in Code: AI and the Future of*

Auditing, p. 185, 198; *The Invisible Revolution*, p. 201)

AI is the science of creating computer systems that perform tasks requiring human-like intelligence, such as problem-solving, perception, or decision-making. Unlike fixed-rule programs, AI systems can learn, adapt, and improve from data. Throughout this book, AI is positioned not as a rival but as a collaborator: a tool to enhance education, healthcare, and industry while sparking vital debates about fairness, ethics, and human dignity in a digital age.

8. Augmented Reality (AR) with AI

(*The Intelligent Journey*, p. 109)

AR enhanced by AI overlays digital information onto the physical world, adapting in real time to context. In travel, it might show historical facts through your phone camera as you explore a monument. In education, AI-driven AR can bring a science lesson to life. By intelligently interpreting surroundings, AR enriches and makes experiences more interactive, although balancing immersion with accuracy and avoiding information overload remains a significant challenge.

9. Autonomy (in AI Systems)

(*Probabilistic AI: Navigating Uncertainty*, p.89, 94; *Stamped in Silicon: When Robots Queue at Customs*, p. 151, 153; *The Invisible Revolution*, p. 211- 229)

Autonomy refers to the degree of independence AI systems exercise in decision-making. From self-driving cars that navigate traffic to audit systems that flag fraud without prompts, autonomy is central to AI's power and risk. Greater autonomy can improve speed and efficiency, but it also creates legal and ethical puzzles about responsibility when errors occur. Defining boundaries for machine autonomy is a recurring theme across many domains in the book.

10. Bayesian Neural Networks (BNN)

(*Probabilistic AI: Navigating Uncertainty*, p. 86)

BNNs extend traditional neural networks by modelling uncertainty directly. Instead of treating network weights as fixed, they represent them as probability distributions, producing predictions alongside confidence estimates. For instance, a BNN diagnosing pneumonia might note high uncertainty due to poor image quality, prompting further human review. This transparency allows safer decision-making in critical areas like healthcare, finance, and autonomous driving, where knowing "what we don't know" can save lives.

11. Bayes' Rule

(*Probabilistic AI: Navigating Uncertainty*, p. 81)

Bayes' Rule is a mathematical formula for updating beliefs when new evidence appears. In AI, it underpins probabilistic reasoning. For example, noticing storm clouds raises the probability of rain compared to a sunny forecast. AI systems use Bayes' Rule to refine predictions in real time, be it medical diagnoses or fraud risk assessments. Its simplicity belies its power: a disciplined way to think under uncertainty and continuously learn from data.

12. Bias (in AI)

(*AI for Rural-Classrooms to Industry-Skilling*, p. 5-31; *Decoding Emotions with AI*, p. 63, 65; *Probabilistic AI: Navigating Uncertainty*, p. 79- 99; *Red Flags in Code: AI and the Future of Auditing*, p. 185-197; *The Invisible Revolution*, p. 216-228)

Bias in AI arises when models trained on incomplete or skewed data produce unfair results, such as misclassifying certain cultural behaviours as risks. Left unchecked, bias can reinforce discrimination in lending, hiring, or education. The book emphasizes governance practices like diverse datasets, bias testing, and community feedback. AI can expand opportunity only if fairness and inclusivity are intentionally designed into its foundations.

13. Chatbot (Conversational Agent)

(*Decoding Emotions with AI*, p. 41-67; *The Invisible Revolution*, p. 105-108)

Chatbots are AI-driven systems that simulate conversation with users. Early bots followed rigid scripts, while modern versions use large language models for fluid, natural dialogue. In healthcare, they offer daily mood check-ins; in travel, they manage bookings and answer questions. Chatbots extend access to services, but also risk over-reliance, shallow empathy, or mishandling crises. Their effectiveness depends on transparency, escalation to humans, and ethical safeguards.

14. Cognitive Behavioural Therapy (CBT)

(*Decoding Emotions with AI*, p. 44)

A type of psychotherapy that helps individuals identify and change negative thought patterns and behaviors. It is evidence-based and commonly used to treat conditions like depression, anxiety, and phobias by encouraging healthier thinking and coping strategies.

15. Computer Vision

(*Decoding Emotions with AI*, p. 45; *Harvesting the Stars*, p. 119-129)

Computer vision is the use of AI to interpret and analyze visual data, such as faces, objects, or movement. In emotion AI, it helps detect stress from facial expressions; in space-based solar projects, it aids robotic swarms in aligning solar panels. By giving machines "sight," computer vision broadens AI's role in healthcare, education, and energy. Yet its accuracy hinges on quality data, and misuse risks surveillance concerns.

16. Continuous Auditing

(*Red Flags in Code: AI and the Future of Auditing*, p. 194)

Continuous auditing uses AI to check transactions in real time, rather than relying on periodic sampling. This allows early detection of fraud, errors, or compliance breaches. For instance, duplicate payments or unusual patterns can be flagged within hours instead of months. Continuous auditing transforms the auditor's role from after-the-fact checker to proactive overseer. However, it also demands strong governance to avoid over-reliance on systems that can themselves fail or misinterpret.

17. Counterfactual Reasoning

(*Probabilistic AI: Navigating Uncertainty*, p. 85)

Counterfactual reasoning is the ability to ask "what if" questions, imagining alternate pasts or outcomes. In healthcare, it might simulate whether earlier treatment would have changed survival chances. For AI, mastering counterfactuals enables better planning, ethics, and causal understanding. Most current models excel at spotting patterns, but struggle with cause-and-effect. Developing this capacity is key for AI systems that must make decisions in uncertain, changing environments.

18. Deep Learning

(*Probabilistic AI: Navigating Uncertainty*, p. 77, 83; *Smarter, Faster, Greener: AI's Role in Sustainable 6G*, p. 176)

Deep learning uses extensive, multi-layer neural networks to uncover complex patterns in massive datasets. It underpins breakthroughs like image recognition, speech translation, and generative art. These systems learn representations automatically, without humans telling them what features matter. While deep learning has powered much of AI's progress, it often lacks explainability, making governance and trust critical when outcomes affect health, finance, or justice.

19. Digital Twin

(*Harvesting the Stars*, p. 130, 131)

A digital twin is a virtual replica of a real-world system, such as a solar power satellite or hospital.

By simulating conditions digitally, engineers can test scenarios, predict failures, and refine performance without risking physical systems. In AI, digital twins combine real-time data with simulation to provide safe, adaptive experimentation. They are central to ambitious projects like space-based solar power, where prototypes are impractical to build physically at scale.

20. DIKSHA

(*AI for Rural-Classrooms to Industry-Skilling*, p. 28)

An Indian government initiative providing a national digital platform for teachers, students, and educational administrators. It offers e-learning content, training resources, and teaching aids in multiple Indian languages to support school education and teacher capacity-building.

21. Dual Blueprint

(*AI for Rural-Classrooms to Industry-Skilling*, p. 4-29)

The Dual Blueprint refers to a strategy combining foundational rural education with advanced industry-specific training, supported by AI storytelling. The idea is that without strong early education, advanced skilling falls flat, and without advanced skilling, education risks irrelevance. AI helps bridge this gap by generating tailored content from village-level science lessons to simulations of industry workflows, creating a pipeline of future-ready learners.

22. EEG

(*Decoding Emotions with AI*, p. 45)

Electroencephalography is a technique used to record the electrical activity of the brain using electrodes placed on the scalp. EEG is commonly used in medical and research settings to study brain function, diagnose epilepsy, sleep disorders, and monitor anesthesia.

23. Electronic Personhood

(*Stamped in Silicon: When Robots Queue at Customs*, p. 147-156)

Electronic personhood is a proposed legal status for highly autonomous AI, granting them limited rights and responsibilities. This status could allow robots to hold digital wallets, sign contracts, or bear liability. While debated in the European Parliament, it remains controversial: critics argue that machines lack consciousness or moral agency. The concept reflects society's struggle to adapt laws designed for humans to increasingly autonomous digital actors.

24. Epistemic Uncertainty

(*Probabilistic AI: Navigating Uncertainty*, p. 84-95)

Epistemic uncertainty arises from a lack of knowledge, either because the model is incomplete or the data is limited. Unlike aleatoric uncertainty (natural randomness), epistemic uncertainty can be reduced with more data or better models. In AI, recognizing this uncertainty is key to building robust systems. For example, a medical AI might flag a diagnosis as uncertain due to insufficient patient data, prompting a doctor to gather more information before deciding.

25. Explainability

(*Red Flags in Code: AI and the Future of Auditing*, p. 193)

Explainability in AI refers to the ability to understand and interpret the reasoning behind an AI model's decisions. This is particularly important in high-stakes domains like healthcare and finance, where opaque, “black box” models can be risky. Techniques for explainability include visualizing model behavior, generating human-readable explanations, and using simpler, more transparent models.

26. Explainable AI (XAI)

(*Red Flags in Code: AI and the Future of Auditing*, p. 216)

XAI includes techniques that make AI's decision-making transparent. Rather than issuing a black-box prediction, XAI shows which factors influenced an outcome. For example, an audit AI might flag fraud and highlight "clustered transactions under approval threshold." By explaining its rationale, XAI builds trust, accountability, and fairness. Clear, plain-language explanations help regulators, professionals, and everyday users interpret AI decisions responsibly.

27. Fairness

(*Decoding Emotions with AI*, p. 65, 69; *Probabilistic AI: Navigating Uncertainty*, p. 94; *Red Flags in Code: AI and the Future of Auditing*, p. 190-198; *The Invisible Revolution*, p. 228)

Fairness in AI means ensuring that AI systems do not perpetuate or amplify existing biases in society. This requires careful attention to the data used to train AI models, as well as the algorithms themselves. Techniques for promoting fairness include using diverse and representative datasets, auditing models for bias, and developing algorithms that are robust to demographic differences.

28. Federated Learning

(*The Invisible Revolution*, p. 210-228)

Federated learning trains AI models across multiple devices without sending raw data to a central server. For example, smart home sensors might improve fall detection models by sharing only learned patterns, not personal details. This preserves privacy while still enhancing accuracy. Used in healthcare and personal assistants, federated learning balances data utility with privacy, though governance is still needed to ensure transparency and avoid hidden bias.

29. Fraud Detection with AI

(*Red Flags in Code: AI and the Future of Auditing*, p. 188-195)

Fraud detection uses AI to analyze transactions for suspicious patterns such as invoice splitting or irregular payment clusters. Unlike manual sampling, AI systems can scan all records continuously, catching red flags early. Human auditors then verify whether flagged cases are genuine fraud or legitimate anomalies. This partnership of machine efficiency with human judgment makes fraud detection faster and more reliable, while also reminding us not to over-reliance on algorithms.

30. Generative AI

(*AI for Rural-Classrooms to Industry-Skilling*, p. 11; *The Intelligent Journey*, p. 105-110)

Generative AI models create new content like stories, images, and voices, based on patterns in training data. Tools like ChatGPT or Midjourney showcase their potential for storytelling, education, and creativity, making high-quality production widely accessible. At the same time, generative AI challenges existing systems of authorship, trust, and ownership. The book positions it as both an opportunity and a responsibility: a tool to democratize creation, provided safeguards and ethics stay central.

31. Governance

(*AI for Rural-Classrooms to Industry-Skilling*, p. 23; Decoding Emotions with AI, p. 69; *Probabilistic AI: Navigating Uncertainty*, p. 94; *Smarter, Faster, Greener: AI's Role in Sustainable 6G*, p. 179; *Red Flags in Code: AI and the Future of Auditing*, p. 186-196; *The Invisible Revolution*, p. 219)

AI governance refers to the development of policies, standards, and practices to ensure that AI is developed and used responsibly. This includes addressing issues of accountability, transparency, and fairness, as well as managing the risks associated with AI. Effective AI governance requires collaboration between researchers, policymakers, and the public.

32. Greener Networks (AI & Telecom Context)

(*Smarter, Faster, Greener: AI's Role in Sustainable 6G*, p. 164, 180)

Telecom infrastructures are designed to minimize energy consumption and carbon emissions through AI-driven optimization. This includes powering down idle equipment, integrating renewable energy sources, implementing predictive maintenance, and traffic-aware management to ensure that future 6G networks are both high-performing and environmentally sustainable.

33. Green Hydrogen

(*AI for Rural-Classrooms to Industry-Skilling*, p. 23)

Hydrogen gas is produced using renewable energy (like solar or wind) through electrolysis of water. It is considered a clean fuel because it does not emit carbon dioxide when burned or used in fuel cells, making it a key element in the transition to sustainable energy.

34. HVAC

(*The Invisible Revolution*, p. 222)

Heating, Ventilation, and Air Conditioning is a system used in buildings and vehicles to regulate temperature, humidity, and air quality. HVAC systems provide thermal comfort and maintain indoor air quality through heating, cooling, and ventilation.

35. Hybrid Delivery

(*AI for Rural-Classrooms to Industry-Skilling*, p. 18)

A hybrid delivery combines AI-powered digital lessons with offline, community-based teaching. For example, animated AI lessons may be shown in schools while mentors lead in-person discussions. This "phygital" approach balances scale with human connection. It ensures students benefit from adaptive digital content without losing the empathy and dialogue that only humans can provide, creating a more inclusive, sustainable education system.

36. Simulation (AI Context)

(*AI for Rural-Classrooms to Industry-Skilling*, p. 6-23; Harvesting the Stars, p. 130, 131)

A method of creating virtual models to replicate real-world processes, environments, or systems. In education, AI-driven simulations immerse learners in realistic industry scenarios for skill training. In engineering, simulations test large-scale projects like space-based solar power under controlled digital conditions before real-world execution.

37. Internet of Things (IoT) with AI

(*The Invisible Revolution*, p. 206)

IoT describes networks of everyday devices, fridges, lights, and wearables, that collect and exchange data. When combined with AI, IoT systems adapt intelligently: thermostats learn usage patterns, smart grids optimize energy flow, and medical sensors monitor health in real-time. The challenge is to manage the vast amounts of data generated and ensure security and privacy. IoT with AI promises a future where technology anticipates needs, making environments more responsive and efficient.

38. Ladder of Causation

(*Probabilistic AI: Navigating Uncertainty*, p. 85)

The “ladder of causation” describes three levels of reasoning: association (spotting patterns), intervention (testing changes), and counterfactuals (imagining alternatives). Many AI systems remain on the first rung, recognizing patterns but not reasoning about cause. Advanced probabilistic AI aims to climb higher, supporting systems that can plan, test, and imagine. This ladder is crucial for domains like medicine or policy, where understanding cause makes the difference between correlation and real insight.

39. Large Language Models (LLMs)

(*AI for Rural-Classrooms to Industry-Skilling*, p. 10; *Decoding Emotions with AI*, p. 46)

LLMs are advanced AI models trained on vast amounts of text data, enabling them to understand, generate, and translate human language with remarkable fluency. Examples include GPT-3 and BERT. They power applications like chatbots, content creation tools, and search engines. While LLMs can produce highly coherent and contextually relevant text, they can also generate misinformation or reflect biases present in their training data. Ethical development and deployment require careful consideration of their limitations and potential societal impact.

40. Machine Learning (ML)

(*Decoding Emotions with AI*, p. 41-54; *Probabilistic AI: Navigating Uncertainty*, p. 85; *The Intelligent Journey*, p. 110; *Harvesting the Stars*, p. 124-129; *Smarter, Faster, Greener: AI's Role in Sustainable 6G*, p. 175, 178; *The Invisible Revolution*, p. 214)

ML is a subset of AI that enables systems to learn from data without explicit programming. Instead of being given fixed rules, ML algorithms identify patterns and make predictions or decisions based on the data they are fed. This allows them to improve performance over time. ML is foundational to many

AI applications, from recommendation systems to medical diagnosis.

41. Multimodal

(*Decoding Emotions with AI*, p. 45; *The Invisible Revolution*, p. 209-227)

The capability of AI systems to process and integrate information from multiple sources (modalities) such as text, speech, images, gestures, or sensor data. In mental health, it combines voice, facial expressions, and physiological signals to interpret emotions. In ambient intelligence, multimodal systems merge visual, audio, and environmental cues for richer contextual awareness and adaptive responses.

42. Natural Language Processing (NLP)

(*Decoding Emotions with AI*, p. 41-54)

NLP is a field of AI that focuses on enabling computers to understand, interpret, and generate human language. It encompasses tasks like translation, sentiment analysis, and text summarization. NLP is the technology behind chatbots, voice assistants, and other applications that allow humans to interact with computers using everyday language.

43. NCERT

(*AI for Rural-Classrooms to Industry-Skilling*, p. 20)

National Council of Educational Research and Training is an autonomous organization under the Government of India that develops curriculum, textbooks, teaching resources, and educational policies for school education in India. NCERT materials are widely used in Indian schools and serve as references for competitive exams.

44. Neural Network

(*Probabilistic AI: Navigating Uncertainty*, p. 83, 86)

A neural network is a type of machine learning model inspired by the structure of the human brain. It consists of interconnected nodes, or "neurons," organized in layers. Each connection has a weight that is adjusted during training, allowing the network to learn complex patterns and relationships in data. Neural networks are used in a wide range of AI applications, including image recognition, natural language processing, and autonomous driving.

45. Neuromorphic Computing

(*The Invisible Revolution*, p. 208-227)

An emerging field of computer engineering that designs hardware and software modeled on the structure and functioning of the human brain. It uses artificial neurons and synapses to enable energy-efficient processing, adaptive learning, and real-time data handling.

46. NGO

(*AI for Rural-Classrooms to Industry-Skilling*, p. 16-31)

A Non-Governmental Organization is a non-profit, voluntary organization that operates independently of government control. NGOs often work in areas such as social development, humanitarian aid, education, health, and environmental protection.

47. Phygital

(*AI for Rural-Classrooms to Industry-Skilling*, p. 18)

Phygital is a term that combines the words "physical" and "digital." It refers to the integration of digital technologies into physical spaces and experiences. In education, a phygital approach might involve using augmented reality to bring textbook illustrations to life or using interactive whiteboards to facilitate collaborative learning.

48. Privacy

(*AI for Rural-Classrooms to Industry-Skilling*, p. 5-31; *Decoding Emotions with AI*, p. 53-70; *The Intelligent Journey*, p. 112; *Stamped in Silicon: When Robots*

Queue at Customs, p. 158; *The Invisible Revolution*, p. 210-229)

Privacy is a significant concern in the age of AI, as AI systems often require large amounts of data to function effectively. It is essential to ensure that this data is collected and used in a way that respects individual privacy. This includes using techniques like data anonymization and federated learning, as well as giving users control over their own data.

49. Probabilistic AI

(*Probabilistic AI: Navigating Uncertainty*, p. 75-98)

Probabilistic AI is a branch of AI that deals with uncertainty. It uses probability theory to represent and reason about incomplete or noisy information. Probabilistic AI models can provide not only a prediction but also a measure of confidence in that prediction, which is crucial for decision-making in high-stakes domains like healthcare and finance.

50. Reinforcement Learning

(*Smarter, Faster, Greener: AI's Role in Sustainable 6G*, p. 173, 174)

Reinforcement learning is a type of machine learning where an agent learns to make decisions by interacting with an environment. The agent receives rewards or penalties for its actions, and its goal is to maximize the cumulative reward over time.

Reinforcement learning is used in a variety of applications, including robotics, game playing, and autonomous navigation.

51. Robot

(*The Intelligent Journey,* p. 103, 108; *Harvesting the Stars*, p. 124; *Stamped in Silicon: When Robots Queue at Customs*, p. 145-159; *Smarter, Faster, Greener: AI's Role in Sustainable 6G*, p. 167; *The Invisible Revolution*, p. 202)

A machine designed to carry out tasks automatically, often programmable to perform simple to highly complex functions. When integrated with AI, robots can act autonomously, adapt to their environment, and even take on roles that blur the line between tool and agent, raising new social, ethical, and legal questions.

52. Robotic Swarms

(*Harvesting the Stars*, p. 131)

A collective of simple robots that coordinate their actions through decentralized control, inspired by behaviors in nature (like ants or bees). In AI applications, robotic swarms are used for large-scale, complex tasks such as assembling solar farms in space, disaster recovery, or environmental monitoring. They rely on autonomy, communication, and collaboration rather than central control.

53. Robustness

(*Harvesting the Stars*, p. 132)

Robustness in AI refers to the ability of an AI system to maintain its performance even when faced with unexpected or noisy inputs. This is important for ensuring that AI systems are reliable and can be trusted to perform well in real-world situations. Techniques for improving robustness include using diverse training data, adding noise to the training process, and developing algorithms that are less sensitive to small changes in the input.

54. Safety

(*AI for Rural-Classrooms to Industry-Skilling*, p. 17, 19; *Decoding Emotions with AI*, p. 47-68; *Probabilistic AI: Navigating Uncertainty*, p. 96; *Harvesting the Stars*, p. 128; *Stamped in Silicon: When Robots Queue at Customs*, p. 148-153; *The Invisible Revolution*, p. 211, 216)

Safety is a critical consideration in the development and deployment of AI systems, particularly those that have the potential to cause physical or emotional harm. It is essential to design AI systems that are safe by default and to have mechanisms in place to prevent them from causing damage. This includes techniques like value alignment, which aims to ensure that the goals of the AI system are aligned with human values.

55. Security

(*Decoding Emotions with AI*, p. 64; *Stamped in Silicon: When Robots Queue at Customs*, p. 145-150; *The Invisible Revolution*, p. 209-221)

Security is another crucial consideration in the age of AI, as AI systems can be vulnerable to attack. It is essential to design AI systems that are secure and to have mechanisms in place to protect them from unauthorized access or modification. This includes using techniques like encryption and authentication, as well as developing AI systems that are resilient to adversarial attacks.

56. Storytelling (with AI)

(*AI for Rural-Classrooms to Industry-Skilling*, p. 4-31)

AI-powered storytelling uses generative AI to create engaging and immersive narratives. This can include generating text, images, and even videos. In education, AI storytelling can be used to create personalized and interactive learning experiences that are more effective and engaging than traditional methods.

57. Transparency

(*Decoding Emotions with AI*, p. 69; *Probabilistic AI: Navigating Uncertainty*, p. 93, 96; *Harvesting the*

Stars, p. 137; *Stamped in Silicon: When Robots Queue at Customs*, p. 153-158; *Red Flags in Code: AI and the Future of Auditing*, p. 187; *The Invisible Revolution*, p. 215-228)

In AI, transparency refers to the ability to see and understand how an AI system works. It is essential for building trust in AI systems and ensuring they are used fairly and ethically. Techniques to promote transparency include clear explanations of how AI systems function, making training data available for inspection, and allowing independent audits of AI systems.

58. Trust

(*AI for Rural-Classrooms to Industry-Skilling*, p. 20-27; *Decoding Emotions with AI*, p. 40-70; *Probabilistic AI: Navigating Uncertainty*, p. 78-97; *Harvesting the Stars*, p. 137; *Stamped in Silicon: When Robots Queue at Customs*, p. 149-159; *Red Flags in Code: AI and the Future of Auditing*, p. 185-198; *The Invisible Revolution*, p. 215, 223)

Trust is essential for the successful adoption of AI. People need to be able to trust that AI systems will be fair, reliable, and safe. Building trust in AI requires a combination of technical solutions, such as explainability, robustness, and social solutions, such as transparency and accountability.

59. Virtual Reality (VR)

(*The Intelligent Journey*, p. 105; *Smarter, Faster, Greener: AI's Role in Sustainable 6G*, p. 167)

VR with AI creates immersive, interactive, and intelligent virtual environments. AI can be used to generate realistic and responsive virtual characters, to personalize the VR experience for each user, and to create more challenging and engaging VR games and simulations. VR with AI has a wide range of potential applications, from entertainment and education to training and therapy.

Index

U

V

W

Y

For Product Safety Concerns and Information please contact our EU representative GPSR@taylorandfrancis.com
Taylor & Francis Verlag GmbH, Kaufingerstraße 24, 80331 München, Germany

www.ingramcontent.com/pod-product-compliance
Ingram Content Group UK Ltd.
Pitfield, Milton Keynes, MK11 3LW, UK
UKHW022155190926
475702UK00003B/39
* 9 7 8 1 0 4 1 2 3 6 9 9 3 *